Women Triumph When Tough Traits Rule

AD 61 to Present

BABETTE ANTON

iUniverse®

WOMEN TRIUMPH WHEN TOUGH TRAITS RULE
AD 61 TO PRESENT

iUniverse books may be ordered through booksellers or by contacting:

iUniverse
1663 Liberty Drive
Bloomington, IN 47403
www.iuniverse.com
1-800-Authors (1-800-288-4677)

Because of the dynamic nature of the Internet, any web addresses or links contained in this book may have changed since publication and may no longer be valid. The views expressed in this work are solely those of the author and do not necessarily reflect the views of the publisher, and the publisher hereby disclaims any responsibility for them.

Any people depicted in stock imagery provided by Thinkstock are models, and such images are being used for illustrative purposes only.
Certain stock imagery © Thinkstock.

ISBN: 978-1-5320-1644-8 (sc)
ISBN: 978-1-5320-1645-5 (e)

Library of Congress Control Number: 2017903021

Print information available on the last page.

iUniverse rev. date: 04/06/2017

In memory of my friend and author Pat Conroy (a Citadel Grad), who supported Nancy Mace as the first female to graduate as a member of the Citadel's Corp of Cadets in Charleston, South Carolina.

Preface

It is fact that women's opportunities have grown because of the courage of a few. Perhaps you already know of one of the women within this book.

Women Triumph asks young females to realize the slow journey forward of women's rights in order not to fall into lives of controlling men. Reading here about tough women's traits should support and lift you when you stand alone.

Becoming familiar with these heroines can strengthen your personal directions now and forever.

1

Boudicca Crushes the Romans to Save Her Iceni Tribe

I f for centuries women had only obeyed men, how would human beings have truly advanced? Historical records provide multiple examples of women who bravely went forward alone to save their people. And so it is written that in AD 61, Queen Boudicca, recognized for her leadership, physically led her British Celtic tribe, the Iceni, against the occupying army of the Roman Empire. She fought for her people in order to save them and their advanced culture from these powerful enemies. Exceptional for certain was that this "mere" woman was fiercely capable of fighting for her people.

More than two thousand years ago, Boudicca, while both wife of the Celtic king Prasutagus and mother to their daughters, surprised the Iceni's frightening enemy soon after they had killed her husband. With this testament of her bravery, the deceased king's wife became the trusted, groundbreaking heroine of her people, and she became frozen in time as the "Warrior Queen Boudicca."

Her actions, supported by her financial inheritance, steadied her position as the queen. There is little doubt that her intent was to drive back her people's enemy and go forward as her husband, King Prasutagus, would have done. And so now with Queen Boudicca having successfully won her first military victory, she prepared again to attack those who waited to wipe out her people. Rather than allow them to converge upon the Celt's Iceni people, this royal female with flowing reddish-blonde hair rode forward in her chariot toward the unsuspecting Roman legions.

Without a whimper or fear, Boudicca and her army rode bravely forward to kill the cocky Romans before they could capture, rape, and kill those she protected. How could history forget this fearless woman? In fact, her story never has completely faded. She was and is remembered as the woman who went against all odds to rid the larger Britannia of the Roman trespassers. The Iceni (one of the Celtic tribes) was one of the few populations that had been left intact while King Prasutagus lived. In fact, the king placated the Romans with money while also directing financial homage to their ruler, Nero. Boudicca's husband, the king, had stood beside and not beneath the Roman invaders. Prasutagus masterfully kept the invaders satisfied by paying homage to their leader, Nero. However, upon his death he left half of his kingdom to the Romans and half to his wife and daughters.

His directed inheritance to these females was totally unheard of and, indeed, unacceptable at the time. Instead, a man's estate for thousands of years would pass only to his eldest son. But there were no sons, and Prasutagus knew Boudicca's abilities.

Clearly history supports Queen Boudicca's strength. She never winced once upon acting against the traditional evil of the Romans in Britannia. In looking back, one must presume that she put aside trepidations to attack the Romans. So swiftly was Boudicca's attack that they were stunned. Indeed, they had prepared to either butcher or enslave her, her daughters, and the entirety of the Iceni people. Instead, the queen led her army against those who also had planned to take the Iceni land.

King Prasutagus's sudden death opened the door in military thinking to act quickly against his family and his people. Who would have thought that his wife, Boudicca, would emerge as the capable, fierce leader she proved herself to be? Apparently nary one among the enemy recognized what was coming. For indeed, the opposing

Romans had not gotten within the thoughts of this strong-willed, fearless woman, whose army charged ahead to beat them back. Yet she led her army, and that is how we know her today.

If tears or fear had ever shown on her lovely face, it has never been recorded. Quite certainly, she knew what she must do when confronted with her long-held, firm understanding of the Romans. Even though Julius Caesar had already left the country, thousands of his soldiers stayed to control Britannia.

And so it is that historians have honored her as an unusual female warrior, who would not allow her heritage or the Iceni people to be removed from existence. In addition, she was sly enough to have allowed the Romans to believe she was a meager, incapable woman, who was fearful and incapable of defending herself and her deceased husband's tribe. How careless of them. For in fact, she was a queen with a military mind. Queen Boudicca was eager to kill thousands of Roman soldiers before they grouped to kill her and her people. As has been written for centuries now, this is just what happened.

However, she was pushed further: The Romans had Boudicca publically flogged and her young daughters raped. Pointedly, such female rapes have remained through the centuries to prevail even today.

To avenge such evil, the heroine Boudicca sought revenge in a brave feat that must be remembered and honored. She rode forward with her army to destroy the confident Romans. Their soldiers must have made many excuses about losing this battle to the Iceni queen.

Along with the Roman governor far to the north, she heroically led her army to the Roman's fortress in Britain. However, she did not stop there. She also burned the city of Camulodunum to the ground, as well as Londinium (London today). Then she charged into Verulamium (St. Albans today). According to estimates, she and her army brutally killed some seventy thousand of those who had killed and maimed the Iceni people. Certainly, Queen Boudicca was tough enough to charge forward until the end. Historic writings left for posterity say that Boudicca killed herself when the Romans overtook her.

Markedly, questions circle her staggering effort to stand against the Romans. However, there is little doubt that she was courageous, strong, intelligent, and tough to the core. What a leader of this army of men against men!

Her memory carried forward, and other royalty through the ages saw strong female traits in themselves. In fact, a statue of Boudicca on her chariot with her daughters is prominent even today on the embankment of Westminster Bridge in sight of Elizabeth I Tower of London. Women who visit for the first time have to be impressed.

In essence, a look at gender roles in free and open countries have preserved the history of this queen. Boudicca set a precedent for others to remember what it takes for women to go forward and win their arguments (or battles) when necessary.

She acted. She sought revenge against the Romans who had beaten her and raped her daughters, won huge battles, and must have known her death would most certainly be the death of a memorable warrior. Although Queen Boudicca killed herself, she knew she had been beaten by her Roman enemy. Did she believe that the Romans would ultimately give up on conquering her people to leave Britannia as Julius Caesar did before them? They withdrew and went back to Italy.

So what character traits stand out within this warrior queen? Boldness, intelligence, and her commitment to her tribe are obvious. Importantly, she didn't allow tears to flow; she didn't run from the enemy; and most significantly, she maintained the courage to fight until she was beaten. For that, she is remembered as a heroine and credited for forcing the Romans from England.

Boudicca will also be remembered because of her fearless mettle. Ultimately, each step forward for women has not only motivated other females but also continues to guide much of the world's women who have been downtrodden, beaten, raped, and killed. Yet still today, huge numbers of men in the United States are arrested every day for committing evil acts against women, tried in court, and sent to prison for those criminal acts.

Queen Boudicca was married to a king. Her husband believed in her abilities and nodded his approval for her pluck when he was still alive. It is easy to imagine that their marriage was a well-centered, successful one. Who could not conclude that King Prasutagus's support of his wife cultivated confidence in her and aided her long-term outcomes?

Boudicca's intelligence and good health, as well as the fact that she never displayed public tears, characterized her as a winner. Importantly, she also was seen to pursue right over might. How fortunate the Iceni knew their queen would support her people and willingly die for them.

2

*E*lizabeth I's Wary Mind Led Her to Protect Herself

Elizabeth I's eyes opened at birth to changes that were rapidly emerging in terms of religion, power, and her own believed illegitimacy. Her father, Henry VIII, and his second wife, Ann Boleyn, were her birth parents. Henry had annulled his marriage to his first wife, Katharine of Aragon, and married Ann. Then to make matters worse, countries on both sides of the English Channel had taken sides between the Catholic Church and history's then forming Reformation. If that wasn't enough, these quickly changing times also involved the invention of the Guttenberg Press and its ability to put thoughts in print, as well as to secretly duplicate and pass forward warring sentiments on religion and government.

Locked in the tower as a child, Elizabeth faced the early possibility of being executed on the chopping block as her mother ultimately had been. Yet instead, she survived and ultimately became the favorite of her people.

Sleeping at night, whether in the Tower of London or in England's famous castle complex, she used her head and carefully stepped back from immediate decision making. She became proficient in three languages and used her expertise carefully.

No one then or today would argue that she did not have

extraordinary intelligence, which in itself led to her eventual popularity with the English people. It is written that Elizabeth studied and waited before making the decisions she was forced to make. And today, who would not guess that deep minds contemplate, listen carefully, and interpret actions as they dance with rivals or smile at antagonists?

Elizabeth often put off making a decision until time had nearly run out, allowed her to have, by then chosen the best for England. Leaders then and now can often be quick to anger and, thus, destroy their arguments and themselves.

However, Queen Elizabeth never hid her femininity or desire to enjoy life. She loved to dance, ride her horses, and dress exquisitely. She had learned her enemies well, and she knew how to slyly handle them. Unfortunately, even as a child, she had feared her half sister Mary as well as Henry's still legitimate wife Queen Katharine. After all, the two had seen the infant Elizabeth as a threat to Mary's own accession to the throne. In fact, many in court privately considered Elizabeth illegitimate since Ann had not been married to the king when Elizabeth was born.

Unable to deal with Mary's hatred of Protestants, Elizabeth discerningly had her half sister executed before her efforts to lead a war against Elizabeth's England could come to fruition. Often, those poisoned with hatred fail, losing their chances to save themselves and missing out on their individual opportunities.

Elizabeth stood tall behind England's defeat of the Spanish Armada, not only with her subjects, but with much of Europe as well.

It is said that she enjoyed the company of men but knew it was she who must rule England. A husband could be an interloper, who more than likely would have attempted to force the queen aside in order to propel himself forward to become England's monarch.

Shrewdly, Elizabeth never wanted to share her popularity or power. And to her population this well-dressed, popular redhead was forever married to England.

In the end, Elizabeth made England a place to watch on the

world's changing map; her country was becoming recognized as an emerging power.

Elizabeth I traveled throughout much of her country each summer so that her people could know, like, and smile upon her with their wholehearted support. Like a traveling show, she wore her stunning clothes and jewelry and allowed her contagious love of England and its recent successes to include the commoners as well. A politician who reached out to those who supported her, she represented their faith in England. For those who threw flowers at her feet, she was their Elizabeth.

At her end, Elizabeth I had served the English people for the entirety of her forty-five years. She lived from 1533 to 1603. Their queen most certainly had led England's Golden Age.

But oh, how she used caution when making decisions. We might, perhaps, compare her to a shrewd player waiting others out in a card game. Apparently, from birth, she had studied well how to survive. Queen Elizabeth I became the symbol of a long-lasting, nearly invincible England.

Despite the fact that thousands of years ago Boudicca and Elizabeth I each had the intelligence to look into her own sturdy character and find a protectress made of steel, many women around the world today are still seen as inferiors, to be owned and controlled by men. History embraced Boudicca and Elizabeth I as females who were lovely outwardly, but as tough as their countries needed them to be.

As the exceptional traits of Queen Elizabeth I developed, she prudently worked to support her people, while she forcefully and successfully enlarged England's position on the world map. She was beyond smart; she was brilliant and calculating. Yet she cherished having a good time, had favorite male friends, and was an equestrian. Because of the way she ruled, Elizabeth was known then and will forever be remembered as an undeniably resilient woman. History is always there to speak for her.

While Elizabeth was still quite young, she was sentenced to the tower. She escaped the guillotine and lived to be venerated for her dynamic leadership.

As no small memory, neither the earlier Boudicca nor Elizabeth I had access to good medicine, running water, toilets, easily accessible fresh food, or decent methods of transportation.

During these times, human life expectancy was much lower than it is today, perhaps around thirty-five years. Additionally, nearly two-thirds of all children died before the age of four. Some light should be shown on the upper classes, who occasionally maintained better health and longer lives because of their access to food and ancient health care. The lives on the lower class were occasionally made even shorter, since they were expected to fight for their lords, although they were often paid and sometimes even knighted. Oh, to the structured outcomes of England's Golden Age.

3

$\mathcal{I}$srael's PM Golda Meir: Recognized and Loved by the World

Often a committed leader, Golda Meir was not immediately seen as a great leader. Yet *steadfast* definitely describes the Golda who led her adopted Israel to prominence. Never youthful or gorgeous, by 1969, at seventy-one years of age, she was elected as Israel's prime minister.

This female prime minister was born in Kiev, Russia, and immigrated first to Germany and later to the United States. In the United States, she graduated from what is now the University of Wisconsin in Milwaukee. She taught there, married, and subsequently moved to Israel, where she and her husband raised a son and a daughter. Strongly in favor of the relatively new state of Israel, she worked somewhat feverishly with this developing country's government.

In time, Golda Meir was elected prime minister of Israel, becoming the third female in the world to hold the position of prime minister. At the same time, she was also recognized as Israel's fourth prime minister, admirably serving her new country from 1969 until 1974.

To lead such a new and struggling country took an unusual personality, vigor, and self-confidence. Golda had it all. Unusual too was her position as a Jewish atheist, even when the world then and now seems to negate leaders who do not abide religious affiliations. And to think that wars are most often fought over religion. Golda simply was the person who the Israelis believed would serve their country best, and so they elected her.

Grandmother to Israel, Golda had served in numerous positions prior to being elected prime minister. Her climb to the nation's top position had earlier included posts as the minister of Internal Affairs, the minister of Foreign Affairs, and the minister of Labor.

Meir put her country above herself. So who could be surprised that the trusted, greatly admired Golda wore orthopedic shoes and kept her gray hair in a granny's bun? If this description of Golda didn't lead Israel and the civilized world to embrace the Israeli prime minister, nothing would. And it did! She prioritized her country's needs over trendy styles or unnecessary socializing.

Prime Minister Golda Meir stood to serve her country. Clearly, she persisted and accomplished much for Israel, along with implementing any changes she deemed necessary.

Meir had the persistence to change what needed to be changed and the tenacity to convince her people that they could be recognized by the world for their intelligence, work ethic, and the tenacity to accomplish.

Because of all of this, the first female prime minister of Israel was labeled the "Iron Woman." Appropriately, she shared her vigorous intensity with the applauding Israelis. Who could not look at that iron-gray hair without noticing Golda's obvious steel within? There, as a participant in the world's leadership, she stood statuesquely to spearhead the success of Israel.

Meir wanted to make Israel secure for Jewish communities to survive, prosper, and give back to the world. She wanted to create a place where, after thousands of years of persecution, the Jewish people would be accepted by humankind for their capabilities, rather than continuing to endure the wide-ranging prejudices so unfairly held against them worldwide.

Unfortunately, antiquity had clung to the vicious hatred of Jews everywhere, with known and unknown enemies pushing a continuous effort to hunt them down and annihilate their race. What demented minds would prey on such gifted, sharp-witted minds?

Perhaps no one can think of a better reason to elect a public official than to realize that she or he will put country before self. Of course, most voters know that the privacy of the inner self can often be hidden from citizens. Prime Minister Meir was rather easy to read. She stood like a woman of iron for the world to acknowledge. And so it was that she both pressed the Israelis to recognize their errors and supported this integrally sewn, often exceptional ethnic group. Meir led her people to contribute their lives to the success of this still developing Jewish homeland.

With her leadership, Golda Meir governed her people by guiding them forward. Beyond a doubt, it was this female prime minister who accelerated Israel forward.

Excitingly too, Israel's prime minister also influenced the futures of capable women everywhere. Few Israelis doubted her passion for Israel's advancing homeland.

Still Golda stood strong for Israel while simultaneously guiding her people to remain on guard against those who, for centuries, had worked to destroy them. These feats took clear reasoning, a certain amount of fearless idealism, devotion to her country, and unusual intellectual wisdom.

PM Meir was loved for her intent to promote the budding Jewish homeland. And although shadowy groups still anticipated toppling Israel, more people around the world became accepting of this young, spirited country. Smartly, she influenced radicals everywhere to tone down hatred in order to secure their own futures.

At the heart of the matter, Prime Minister Golda Meir's resolute character and realistic goals served Israel well. She proudly served her people through three terms of office. To the world, she was the first Iron Lady.

4

Margaret Thatcher, "the Iron Lady": She Simply Had Grit!

L ike Meir, Prime Minister Margaret Thatcher is also remembered as an Iron Lady; and she was most definitely in power when her country needed that kind of leadership. Today, it is vital for present generations everywhere in the Western world to remember that it was Margaret who stood up to the Soviet Union and saved many of the people who had been locked into the Soviet Eastern Bloc of tyranny.

Essentially, Mrs. Thatcher was a fighter with the ability to outlast her enemies. In 1982, she sent her navy to save England's Crown colony in the Falkland Islands off the coast of Argentina. The British won when Argentina surrendered, and Thatcher was popularly reelected the following year.

Indeed, Thatcher's example showed the world that accomplished females can be hard-hitting when defeating their transgressors; or in fact, acknowledging too that not only males can provide successful governance?

Thatcher was quickly perceived as a woman in charge! Here was a female who admitted that her adrenaline flowed when someone wanted to diminish her principled wisdom or well-thought-out plans for her country and the British people.

Thatcher was the daughter of a grocer, which must have made an early imprint on her conservative thinking. Simply speaking, she counted her money carefully and did not believe in wasteful spending. One should sit back for a minute to wonder whether any government today would think twice about wasteful spending. Indeed, often the opposite is true.

With Thatcher's birthright of logical thinking and intense resolve, she was accepted at seventeen years old to Oxford University. She graduated with honors in chemistry, became both a chemist and a tax lawyer, and ultimately married and had children. She had accomplished all of this before being elected as England's prime minister.

Incredibly, Thatcher knew never to lean on someone else. Instead, she would return to herself for all of her final decision making. She was, by no means, a casual leader. Although she had plenty of enemies, Margaret Thatcher stood behind what she believed, no matter how uncompromising her foes wanted to suggest she could be. Unlike many strong-minded female or male leaders, Thatcher selectively chose her battles and most often won them.

Margaret's husband knew exactly who he'd married. With Dennis, Thatcher had two children and a pleasant, agreed on understanding of her objectives.

Rising politically, she sought the male mind and shared political objectives with US president Ronald Reagan. Together, their leadership stood to renounce the Soviet Union's socialist experiment. Their joint goal was to eliminate "that wall" that divided East and West Berlin. And when President Ronald Reagan looked to the east toward the Soviets, he forcibly told the Russians to "Bring down that wall." He acknowledged that he and Margaret Thatcher had together planned their course of action and praised her contributions. The two were surely compatriots. And oh, how joyfully the world received the news of the falling of the Berlin Wall.

Prior to this change, the Eastern Bloc had planted land mines that would explode if any desperate sole attempted to make it over the wall to the West. Many visualized making that journey in order to seek asylum in West Berlin. Shockingly, those trying to escape over the wall were killed as they ran toward freedom.

When East Germany did at last respond by bringing down the wall, no one could miss that the Reagan/Thatcher partnership had worked—that conjointly the two had worked to see that East and West would come together as one Germany. Soon, the world realized that US president Ronald Reagan and English prime minister Margaret Thatcher had labored together to make Germany whole again.

If ever there were two world leaders whose partnership had brought about promising success, it had to have been Thatcher and Reagan. Both fought for years, condemning the separation of Germany's eastern and western halves and the imprisonment of those in East Germany, where communist socialism was forced on those within its borders. Who could deny that the partnership of Thatcher and Reagan stood up to tyranny and triumphed?

Margaret Thatcher, following Golda Meir as the second Iron Lady, died at age eighty-seven after three terms in office. The free world must remember this leader's guidance, determination, and ability to take a tough stand when she was so desperately needed.

In addition, Thatcher was known for having announced England's influence on the globe again and celebrated in her time for saving the British economy. What an elegant woman Thatcher was. She always appeared stylish and attractive. And fortunately, she continuously refused to back down!

Inevitably, she brought Britain from the brink of disaster, as the country had slipped and fallen to the takeover of labor union politics. Her path rocketed the country to a free market economy, which produced jobs, hope, and success.

Characteristic of other great female leaders, Thatcher was convincing in her revolt against socialism and stood behind principled, uncompromising leadership. Essentially, she was a healthy woman who needed few hours of sleep. She wrote and developed her ideas well past the midnight hour and was able to sell the English population on her far-reaching ambitions for the country's immediate development and future.

Strength can draw one to it like a sparkling jewel, or it can instead drive people to turn their heads quickly and walk away. Thatcher relied on exacting calculations. She was extremely purposeful when ensuring those close to her understood and accepted her plans.

Working to steadfastly present her solid thinking, PM Margaret Thatcher burned the midnight oil in order to construct doable decision making. She convinced her constituents to help her save England and England's economy by crossing to her side of the United Kingdom's government. After all, no leader acts alone.

5

$\mathcal{A}$ngela, with the Mettle to Lead: Once Imprisoned behind the Wall

Never Angela who? Because Merkel was suddenly a beacon to follow. After all, by 2014, Angela Merkel was the leader of the European Union, as well as being recognized as the longest-serving elected head of government in Europe. Astonishing, for certain!

Oh, how she succeeded there; quickly the traits that other national leaders saw in her became necessary to their own survival. Merkel's fused Europe Union accelerated quickly toward astonishing progress. And as times changed, more and more female talents were welcomed to the union.

The wide-reaching European countries had early expectations, which quickly developed into solidarity. Merkel undoubtedly contributed to the union of those twenty-eight countries, which, along with their leaders, threw their power behind her. In 2015, at sixty years old, Merkel handled her private and public lives so deftly that governments outside the European Union must have gasped with disbelief or perhaps even with fear of her unifying genius.

And she was a woman at that! Like Margaret Thatcher, Merkel

also was a scientist before she entered politics. She graduated from the University of Leipzig in 1978 with a degree in physics and physical chemistry, while also earning a PhD in quantum chemistry.

As often pointed out, one's environment and genetics often enable individual successes. Time and time again, scholarly females (and males) have possessed the strength to tackle the world's most problematic situations.

Angela was born in West Germany. However, by the end of World War II, lines had been drawn that placed the then Angela Dorothea Kasner within East Germany. Her father was a Lutheran minister, while her mother taught both English and Latin. Perhaps the influence of her early life played a role in the steadfast integrity she was known for.

As her adult world evolved, she married and lived with Ulrich Merkel from 1972 to 1982. Later divorcing, she subsequently married chemistry professor Joachim Sauer in 1998 and became active in politics.

Then, with the fall of the Berlin Wall in 1989, Merkel quickly became steeped in politics. Undoubtedly, her family background, education, inherent intelligence, and clear ability to lead were the fabric that enabled her to become a political front-runner.

She had soon accumulated many titles, and today, the list is huge. Perhaps she has had enough success to garner her reputation as somewhat of a leadership saint.

Merkel has had tremendous successes as she has led the European Union's many countries to the forefront of the world's decision making. Yet, in 2015, Merkel quickly recognized that she'd made a mistake by allowing unvetted refugees to cross into European Union countries. This decision was certainly not happily accepted. However, she indicated she would turn that decision around quickly. Unfortunately, even that did not go smoothly. The one world theory often erupts into deep problems.

At home, Angela learned how to quietly enjoy a few German traditions privately. Outside of the limelight, this nearly invincible leader enjoys cross-country skiing, bakes, and loves soccer. A unique thing about her is that she needs only two hours of sleep a night—much like Margaret Thatcher. And during those cloistered hours, she relishes reading. Apparently, this often means taking in Fyodor Dostoyevsky's (1821–1881) multiple novels, which by all literary standards offer provocative thinking and rereading.

Angela Merkel stands out today as the modern world's governing example of feminine success. As is true of multiple other female leaders, she had the strength and talent to rise to the top of her government. However, along with her achievements, she makes time for privacy and personal choices—an unquestionably difficult feat!

The same is true of many leaders—Margaret Thatcher for example. Thatcher's limited need for sleep allowed her to work at home late at night. She kept that information so private that it enabled her to escape an attempt on her life. One night, she just happened to be up late working and not asleep in her bedroom as the IRA had thought she would be. Consequently, the IRA failed its attempt to kill her with a bomb, which did explode in her bedroom. But this attempt on her life serves as a reminder: Regardless of praise, commitment, or acknowledged success, no leader ever will please everyone or hold a prominent place forever.

If Merkel made an error when she allowed a huge flow of unvetted refugees to cross into her formerly sequestered borders, it must have been an emotional one. And how could that be for Merkel, so often seen to be steady?

Could Merkel's error have been a huge mistake somehow connected to her life as a child in that East German sector? There, of course, most citizens were never allowed to leave. Instead, the communist thinking was dedicated to stopping any of those enslaved from escaping "that wall" lined with explosives, along with soldiers willing to shoot to kill.

Perhaps that was what caused her to make the decision now seen as a bad one; only time will spell out what happens in the long run.

Time will certainly tell. Unfortunately, in 2016, Britain exited the European Union—proving that "nothing stays, everything flows."

6

*B*eautiful Bhutto Assassinated! A Pakistani Female Who Led Change

W hen men assassinate women leaders, they must surely think well of themselves. Perhaps writer Germaine Greer understood that when she wrote, "The tragedy of machismo is that a man is never quite good enough." He must do more!

Benazir Bhutto, the prime minister of Pakistan for two nonconsecutive terms, from 1988 to 1990 and from 1993 to 1996, stood strong for the political party by which her father, Zardari, had been elected and later executed in 1993. Later, her brother was shot and killed in 1996. Attempts at changing the history of the Middle East then and now remain frail, even among relatives.

PM Benazir Bhutto's forward thinking came from her superior education, followed by her desire for reasonable changes in Pakistan. Those in the Western world who championed Bhutto's pursuit remained concerned about her undertaking. They admired her but were concerned about the earlier executions in her family, as well as continuing threats against her. Undoubtedly, the Pakistani leader accepted that she most likely would become a target.

Bhutto's forward policies were in conflict with thousands of still held ancient Muslim rules. With her plans to pursue change, the beautiful Benazir stepped out publicly, dressing according to her own dress code. This choice aggravated those who believed she meant to incite other Muslim women to disobey the ridged controls that governed their clothing. Bhutto's threatening apparel simply included a loose pink headscarf and lipstick! However, Muslim men had made the rules for women to obey for centuries.

At this time in the Western world, reaching defiantly to attack others' religious beliefs were seen occasionally in the past. Certainly things change, yet today the majority of women and men share do not obey buts her decision making.

ISIS (in the state of Iraq and Syria) continues to hold both women and men to their age-old rules, which insist that women obey men.

However, Benazir Bhutto went forward for her family and for the Pakistani people. She hoped to be elected again in order to provide better lives and opportunities for the Pakistani people regardless of their gender.

Bhutto took her chances and returned to Pakistan from England, even though her father and brother had both been assassinated in Pakistan. A third brother was also killed, although he was living in an apartment on the Riviera. When her family members and supporters around the world learned that she had ultimately been assassinated, they undeniably remembered the deaths of her three male family members.

By running again for Pakistani minister, Bhutto hoped to win the election and finalize her plans for a more open Pakistani government.

Yet, al-Qaeda had already arranged for her death as soon as she returned from exile in Dubai. Benazir had hoped to again lead her country, serving for a third term as prime minister. Greeted by huge, welcoming crowds, she must have felt her plans for change awaited her and her applauding supporters just around the corner.

Benazir graduated from Harvard University (though in truth, like all other female students on the Cambridge, Massachusetts, campus, she attended Radcliffe College for women). After completing her degree at Harvard, she continued her education at Great Britain's

Oxford University, where she was a member of St. Catherine's College and lived in Lady Margaret Hall.

To complete her hopes for other Pakistanis, the married mother of three bravely returned to her country to lead again. Her goals if elected were to provide better health, protect women from domestic violence, and promote nutrition and immunization where needed.

Instead, after eight years in exile, she, along with 136 other people, were unmercifully killed in 2007 in a suicide attack.

In the lawless Pakistani tribal region—infested with hatred of her outspoken modernity, her political plans, and her obvious popularity—she seemed a bit too comfortable.

Did she hear whispers that her foes were ready to kill her and send her beloved country backward into the dark ages?

Certainly these Muslim fanatics had shouted out warnings toward many people, but most often they threatened women. And while such widening thoughts went forward, she failed to recognize the depth of her enemies.

Perhaps not wanting to acknowledge her enemy, she failed to see that the rigid rules of Sharia law were to hold—even if that meant continuing to force all females to be covered, conquered, and owned by men as if they were animals. Bhutto, who stood out with her bright mind and red lipstick, was a perfect target for these Muslim killers. In fact, those who ended her life believed such killings were their religious duty. Common to those who wanted no change in the region, they joyfully went forward to kill this brilliant, beautiful, returning female leader.

Whether within families or countries, leading change can often mean unbelievable carnage. In the case of Bhutto, things had changed too much when she returned to her plans for Pakistan.

Bhutto had a strong political background and an exacting past (recall her two prior terms as Pakistani prime minister). She was confident in the predictions that her reelection was a strong possibility, and she willingly returned to the risk of assassination. Benazir Bhutto, with her beautiful smile and the backing of a huge portion of the Pakistani population, braved a return from her personal exile to lead her people. Yet, waving good-bye after speaking to an applauding audience, she stepped up into her well-guarded vehicle with a sunroof. Pleased with her supportive crowd, she stayed to wave to her excited supporters.

Immediately, she was hit with a great number of bullets. She fell and was rushed to a hospital, where she died.

Taken by surprise by those who hated her (her attackers apparently hid their intent behind positive cries among her welcoming crowd), she was doomed before she waved her good-byes. Perhaps she hid her personal fear behind her smiles. But fear alone could not stop her from returning to her beloved Pakistan. She believed she could make a difference in a place where evil dictates keep women in the back rooms, and many men believe Mohamed called for only Muslim men to lead.

Like so many other compelling female leaders, Benazir Bhutto's strength of character, love of country, and desire to initiate better lives for the Pakistani people fortified her. She returned home with hopes of again being reelected as prime minister. Although she was recognized as Pakistan's first female prime minister, she knew danger awaited her, whether she was elected or defeated. And on December 27, 2007, she stood smiling, as she believed her goal was materializing in front of her.

Daughter, wife, mother of three, and twice-elected prime minister, Bhutto had returned to her native country in order to lead it forward. Obviously, she had a steadfast determination and a deep love for Pakistan, its people, and its future. For this, she died!

$\mathcal{I}$ndia and Gandhi in Transition: Killed by Her Trusted Guards

I ndia as one country had been ruled as a parcel of the British Empire. Then in 1947, following the end of World War II, India moved to break away from that two-hundred-year dictate. Almost without warning, India wanted independence from the British. As one would expect, this choice to leave the British Empire did not come easily.

Religions in India included the Church of England, Hinduism, and Islam. The Indians had had enough of Britain's control of their country. However, the British, perhaps in hindsight, must have believed they could control this growing discontent. How could the British powers not have seen that what was brewing in the region was a revolution ready to begin?

As the people of India looked forward to taking back their country, they also had in mind taking neighboring Pakistan and the newly created Bangladesh. War broke out, as they must have anticipated it would.

Had the Indian government thought deeply enough? Would they, having stood united, now fall divided?

Indira Gandhi, then a young woman, feared such upheaval but agreed to participate in India's new direction. Like Bhutto, Gandhi boldly sought revenge against those who had assassinated her father. Proudly, as his only child, she was elected to become the first female prime minister of India.

Popular there, she led and held onto power in India for twenty years, during which she was praised as a legitimate, capable leader in both the Middle East and around the world. However, Gandhi was viewed as a female, regardless of her individual competence and fertile brain. So it was that even she had to struggle for access and recognition in a man's world.

Consider that the demands placed on any leader, female or male, are beyond most people's range of familiarity or experience. It is no surprise, then, that trouble can be instigated without the larger population recognizing it.

Indira went on to marry and became the mother of three children, which meant being involved with her family's life, as most elected women are expected to be. She seemed to have it all, as well as ambitions for India's future.

Much like Pakistan's Benazir Bhutto, Indira also earned early university degrees in England—getting an education there was more likely than in other parts of the Western world, given that Pakistan and India both had been part of that British Commonwealth. Unfortunately, she and Bhutto also shared the same fate. Gandhi was assassinated in 1984, Bhutto in 2007. However, somewhat worse, it was Indira's own trusted Sikhism guards who killed her.

She was said to have ruled with a strong hand, which was most likely necessary in order to control those with poor knowledge of the need for change—change Indira deemed as necessary for her people's own well-being. So often in history, assassins convince themselves to kill those with new ideas. When they see someone who thinks differently, they look at assassination as a simple solution that will return the decision-making power to them.

Should genuine leaders not devote themselves to their countries like they do their families? They publically accept both short- and long-term responsibilities, which include prudently selecting those who will both follow and serve them.

Still, female leaders can be hated for displaying abilities more often attributed solely to male leadership. While gender differences still influence a multitude of choices, one must accept that no one gender is singularly superior in all tasks—unless it is that of birthing babies.

Looking in the mirror once more, before either Gandhi or Bhutto had stepped forward to meet their public, their courage apparently lifted each of them beyond death threats. How often do public figures press forward despite continued threats against them? The public may never know.

The worst of all is to be a traitor to a good leader and to your country. It should not have been that Indira's long trusted bodyguards, who walked beside her as usual on that fatal morning, would be the men who were sent to kill her. They were in a place of honor, looked up to, and carefully chosen to protect her. They didn't even have to be good shots. Two of them simply pulled their guns and shot her dead. Then, just as quickly, they were killed.

In either case, did the assassins' expectations fulfill their need to kill and be killed? Or were they quickly shot and killed in order to erase the truth about those who really supported Gandhi's (and later Bhutto's) assassination? Looking back, it seems clear that disdainful groups high in India's government had to have been behind the assassination.

Irrefutably, both Bhutto and Gandhi had bravely hoped to lead their people toward new-world futures, which would have meant others in high places being eased out. Change should not compel the spilling of blood, although history attests that it does just that far too often. However, it is certain that some individuals will never be satisfied to be led by others, even those with the best intentions for change.

Despite leaders like Gandhi and Bhutto, much of the world continues to begrudge female leaders. In 1990, Indira Gandhi was voted the strongest female leader in the world! Why, at that time, couldn't she simply have been voted the strongest *leader* in the world? Why was the restricting adjective *female* placed in front of her honor?

Privately fearful but born to be strong, Indira Gandhi knew what it would take to be elected. She was committed to her goal and took her chances. Of course, the willingness to take reasonable risks also says a lot about a person. She trusted her bodyguards to die for her. But trust should never be widely held. Leaders must keep an ear to the ground and their eyes to the left and right of them. Compliments and applause can definitely be misleading.

Indira's bright mind and excellent education allowed her to think that her leadership would push India's people forward. She must have pondered privately who it would be best to keep close to her. She must never have believed her guards could be her assassins. Simply put, all leaders must face the possibility of assassination, whether the plot against them come from those closest to them or from sources never known.

Indira Gandhi still speaks out to the world as we read and remember her. We who have studied history must ask questions about those who might attempt to overthrow our own government. Consider the assassinations of former US presidents Abraham Lincoln (the sixteenth president), James A. Garfield (the twentieth president), William McKinley (the twenty-fifth president), and John F. Kennedy (the thirty-fifth president). Each assassination was provoked by changing times.

Reliably, both good people and dreadfully bad people usually have a head start on their plans. In most cases, both environment and genetics play a role. It takes the Secret Service, the Federal Bureau of Investigation, or a wealth of law enforcement in the United States to stop those determined to kill elected officials.

Indira Gandhi simply thought she had unfailingly loyal guards, when in fact, those guards were to be her assassins. She failed from the moment she believed in them and died because of that trust. Trust can be comforting, but it's seldom reliable.

8

Malala, Shot Yet Alive: A Girl on a School Bus

The most recent heroine known in much of the advanced world has been Malala Yousafzai. Ultimately, this thirteen-year-old Pakistani girl only asked that girls be allowed to attend school alongside their male counterparts.

Predictably, she was shot in the head by a Taliban male who meant to kill Malala for her earnest push toward female education. Never foolish but definitely brave, Malala wrote on a blog managed by the BBC that spread her hopes for female equality in education, without disclosing her location or name. However, she was discovered by beastly men who believed they should control not only their women, but even young girls who went against their belief systems. These men accept as true that all uncooperative girls and women should be killed.

In 2012, a faceless man boarded Malala's school bus, which she was determined to ride to school. Her father owned schools for young children to attend in their village on that notorious northeastern edge of Pakistan where Saddam Hussein once hid.

The Brits, prior to Malala's decision to continue in school, were looking for an undisclosed blogger to write about the medieval treatment of females in Pakistan. The plucky Malala insisted on blogging her personal (but unidentified) disappointment that girls were outlawed from attending school.

How she was discovered as the young, intelligent girl whose powerful words fought against such female discrimination is not clear. Yet, clearly her resolve to change this ancient thinking went forward. The prevailing backward thinking Malala pushed back against kept women beasts of burden to be owned, monitored, and repressed by overseeing husbands or male family members.

The brave, dark-eyed child in a pink headscarf was taken down on a simple school bus by a coward with his face covered, who stepped up into the bus with an AK-47 to unhesitatingly ask for Malala Yousafzai.

Bravely, she stepped from her seat to the aisle of the bus. The two looked at each other for seconds before the bandit shot her three times. One of her would-be assassins bullets hit her head and traveled down and through her face to her jawline.

This man attempting murder was surely confident he would be honored by Allah and made a hero. Instead, he went into hiding, and she survived! Subsequently, during her recovery, Malala was told she'd become a heroine, while the shooter had gone into hiding.

Physicians in Pakistan provided immediate medical attention and stabilized Malala. As soon as possible, she was flown to the best emergency medical doctors in England. Saving Malala essentially brought out the truth about men's behavior in countries where women are viewed as their possessions.

Fortunately, the majority of men and women in advanced countries do not hold to such ignorant police. They have struck down these horrendous behaviors that were accepted years ago. Now there are women's shelters to help women escape when men hurt them in order to feel virile. The tragedy of machismo is that often "the man is never quite enough," according to author and feminist Germaine Greer.

Malala's strength has been mighty. She was seen worldwide receiving her 2014 Nobel Peace Prize, as well as asking the world to stand up for children. At the time she was honored in Stockholm, she was just seventeen years old. Beside her there in Sweden was the corecipient of the honor, Kailash Satyarthi, who also received the illustrious Nobel Peace Prize for being a child's rights activist working against child labor in India. What huge risks both had taken in order to change life-threatening situations putting children at great risk.

Malala has continued pushing for the rights of girls in East Pakistan, while feeling her own pulse quicken in step with the danger the Taliban poses to her. However, her desire to right a wrong—the inability of her country's females to read, learn, and succeed—has forced her fear aside. Weighing the threat of death, she campaigned for young Pakistani females to be educated.

Malala would not back down from her fierce opposition—would not give in to those Pakistanis who keep women and children as their property. Intelligent for certain, she remains to bolster educational opportunities for women. She has continued to fight the bigotry of those Pakistani males who believe that women should be ruled by men.

Perhaps the Taliban and its kind will one day end the practice of putting bullets in the heads of those who do not believe in their dogmatic rules. Yet there most likely will never be another child as fearless as Malala, who stood to face the masked man on the bus when he called her name. She knew what was coming but did not back down from him or the Taliban's evil intention to kill her. The result— Malala being flown to England, where her life was saved, and later being able to tell her story on a global stage—was clearly anything but what the Taliban killer had believed would happen when he put a bullet in her head.

How small this evil man must have felt when Malala ultimately received the Nobel Prize. Unfortunately, it is more than likely that this example is not yet enough to change laws for the better or end such savage behavior. But it is a beginning!

9

*A*nne Frank: The Jewess Who Still Believed People Are Really Good of Heart

A nne Frank, one day away from her thirteenth birthday, went with her father, Otto, to a bookstore in Amsterdam, where he bought her the diary she wanted. This happy occasion was on June 12, 1942, and Anne wrote her first entry into that diary on June 14, 1942.

Then so much suddenly changed. Although the family had already gone into hiding in the attic above the warehouse, they feared being found and sent to a prison camp. Then, on July 5, her older sister, Margot, was summoned to appear in a Nazi work camp, where she went. Reading the despicable intent of the Nazi police state, the rest of the family decided to stay secreted in the warehouse annex next to her father's business, where non-Jewish friends kept them hidden.

The beautiful Netherlands now must be remembered for what it was in 1942—and particularly for the laws that were then laid down, which applied only to Jewish people. Otto Frank had already had to give away Anne's bicycle to a Christian family because Jews were suddenly no longer allowed to own bicycles. In addition, they were not allowed to drive their own cars, go to movies, or attend any kind of entertainment.

Already those in Amsterdam were only permitted to shop between 3:00 p.m. and 5:00 p.m. and were not allowed outside in public between 8:00 p.m. and 6:00 a.m.

Anne's diary seemed to save her in this sequestered, uncomfortable hideaway. She had lived there with her eight attic roommates until her sister was called to appear in that Nazi camp. Also hiding in the attic along with the three other Franks were the three Van Pelts and eventually a dentist named Fritz Pleffer. All were found two years and one day from the time they went into hiding. Each person was arrested and taken to a detention camp.

Historic records show that only Anne's father survived this imprisonment and death. He was liberated by American soldiers in late 1944. In the end, the six others who had been taken from the once hidden annex were no longer living.

Of course their being found there above the Franks' warehouse meant someone had learned they were there and turned the families into the Nazi government in the Netherlands. This person had to have been somewhat close to the hidden families in order to reveal their hiding place. Most likely, dislike of Jews and the hopes of a financial reward stood behind the culprit's move.

For those years in the second story of the warehouse, the hideaway was concealed simply by a chest of drawers. Anne and these who hid with her fearfully and cautiously survived, until they were discovered, seized, and sent to different concentration camps.

Of those who had been hidden by the Franks' Christian friends, only Anne's father was alive with the defeat of Nazi Germany and the end of World War II. When the Allied soldiers found and liberated those still barely alive in the evil death camps, they were shocked to learn how many had died there.

The original eight people in hiding became seven when Margot was called early to report to a camp. The others, who lasted for two years and one day, were completely dependent on the supplies brought to them, while hoping beyond hope that somehow the hatred of Jews would end before they were found.

Anne died from typhus before her body was discovered in a

death camp. She was fifteen years—and a day—old and so close to becoming the writer she most definitely would have been had she survived. Among her other belongings was a long list of short stories she'd written while alive and struggling to understand those who were morally empty and heartless.

Those who pressed Otto Frank to publish Anne's diary and other writing understood her talent. The writing was filled with heart and intellect.

To read *The Diary of Anne Frank* means remembering particularly what she had written: "In spite of everything, I believe that people are really good at heart."

How utterly important it is that her writing eventually was made available to excited readers in many nations!

Successful women now know how to deal with adversity, yet perhaps few as well as the child Anne Frank did. Anne had the strength of mind to encounter the threats of her circumstances. In all cases of young girls, their abilities and astounding bravery proves them capable of standing beside history's strongest women.

In Anne's situation, she chose mind over matter, writing in her diary regardless of her circumstances. That included her time in the hidden annex, where she was found and taken separately on her trip to the frightful Bergen-Belsen concentration camp. Then, close to the end of the Third Reich's power, she was moved yet again from the Westerbork transit camp to Auschwitz, where, if she had not died of typhus just two weeks prior to the British troops liberating the camp, she might have lived.

For certain, Anne Frank made the most of her life, due to her faith in her staying power and her attitude toward her circumstances. Most significantly, she unknowingly died to become one of the best-known writers in history. *The Diary of Anne Frank* made her not only the journalist she hoped to be, but also one of the most read literary authors.

Anne Frank had faith in herself, a bright mind, a goal she believed she could reach, and enthusiasm for understanding what could make the world a better place. Despite all she had endured, she went to her death holding positive thoughts about most people.

10

Sybil Ludington, Nearly Forgotten, Traveled Faster and Farther Than Paul Revere

To believe that demeaning, gender-specific references (as when a man blatantly refers to his wife as "the little woman") kept females once dependent on a man's subjugation of them now may appear to be silly or simply ignorant. Yet a look back at history reminds women of what once was.

Heroines and heroes have always lived among us, but oh, how long it has taken for much of the world to accept that there are tough, courageous, intelligent females who must be seen and honored for their own successes. In the case of fifteen-year-old Sybil Ludington, it took centuries for her to be known and perhaps stand next to, if not above, Paul Revere.

In 1777, the young Sybil helped save her state and the entirety of the early thirteen colonies from becoming British. Although Paul Revere is best known for his midnight ride to warn the villages, "The British are coming," it was Sybil who volunteered to make a longer, more dangerous midnight ride when her father was warned of the enemy's intent to attack their town. Frustrated, Lt. Col. Ludington had just returned with his soldiers from an exhausting revolutionary battle they had lost. Both the British and the settlers were on the verge of either winning or losing what is now known as the Revolutionary War. Both sides were worn out and weakened. And in the case of those sleep-deprived soldiers, Ludington had taken them to his farm to rest and prepare for the next battle.

Putting her fear aside, while acknowledging the fate of the colonies would be on her back, Sybil asked her dad to allow her to take on this task. She was a talented rider and looked to her father for the answer. He believed that if those spread out in the hinterlands were warned of the British threat, the settlers would have a chance of winning the war. Their being warned in the middle of the night to grab their guns and horses because "The British are coming" might just mean the end of the war. Knowing his child's capabilities with horses, Ludington had faith that she could assemble the men quickly enough to stand up to the British. And so, with his permission, she rode some forty miles through heavy storms and at the risk of being captured and killed.

Like the many men who risked life and limb to liberate the colonies from the British, the fifteen-year-old Sybil jumped on her favorite horse to save the colonies. Getting caught by the enemy was no small possibility, but it was one she ignored. As she urged the horse with only a small stick, the two of them rode the faster-than-fast pace throughout the settlements. Knocking on each door, she yelled, "The British are coming," and then rode on. After all, the British were on their way to take the colonists' homes and children, while the stalwart settlers' hopes were to win this last battle in order to establish the United States of America.

Sybil, Ludington's oldest child, was known for training horses, making soap, and taking care of her brothers and sisters. Yet she was kept from attending school because she was female. Boys did attend school. Perhaps she was simply waiting to demonstrate her capability, though, like other females, she had been held back simply because she was seen as one of the "weaker sex." How often that mistake must have been made!

Now suddenly Sybil was the Revolution's sole solution. And so it was that she jumped on her horse and rode off into the thunderous rain and darkness. Visiting home after home, she awakened the men, who immediately got their guns and took off to meet the British soldiers head-on. As she continued riding and calling out these warning, she knew the local farmers turned soldiers would give up their lives to defeat the Redcoats. Yes, the young Ludington girl led these men to join the battle that won the American Revolution!

Unfortunately, she was soon forgotten. She was never remembered in the manner of Paul Revere, although his ride was shorter and safer. Unthinkable yet true, no female at this time in American history was to be lauded for saving her country, regardless of the risks she took and her ultimate success.

In 1939, New York State erected a number of markers along her route. Others eventually followed in Washington, DC; Danbury, Connecticut; and at Brookgreen Gardens in Murrells Inlet, South Carolina.

At the time, Sybil simply went home to take care of her sisters and brothers and to one day marry and have a child. And why did it take so long to put her in the pages of history? Apparently nothing was recorded because she was a female. Could it be that Paul Revere would not have wanted her success to be known?

Unfortunately, a woman's lesser status still remains true in many countries today. At the time of the American Revolution, Sybil was a brave trendsetter. As she was so brave and unusual for her time, her memory can now shed light, not only on her heroic accomplishment but also on the cultural acceptance of talented females.

Of course it must be noted that the women's liberation movement did not flourish until the 1980s in the United States. Although the idea floundered a bit then, it continued to move hearts and minds in the United States and other places across the globe.

Today, it must be held sacred that all Americans have opportunities to prove their worth. However, it goes without saying that access to success for any human should depend on her or his abilities and not simply on a gender classification.

It was Sybil Ludington's idea to convince her father to allow her to ride ahead to save the struggling miles of farming families who had to be told that the British were advancing. Even with the possibility of his daughter being caught and killed by British soldiers, Ludington allowed Sybil to go into that dark, rainy night to warn the settlers. And he agreed quickly, for he knew she had what it took to succeed. Yes, even then, many fathers knew that it could take a girl like Sybil to successfully perform a risky task like Sybil's ride. It is often true now that successful girls grow up close to their fathers. The heroic actions of girls are now applauded in hundreds of situations. And in higher education in many parts of the world, women and men now excel equally. How awful that isn't a universal fact.

Sybil knew when not to react, but she clearly acted when she could make life-saving changes. Succinctly put, tough females then and today have an inner resiliency that often enables them to handle difficulties as well as, if not better than, many men.

Learning the concept of danger but overcoming one's fears is not specific to gender but to the individual. And so Sybil Ludington is remembered! She was definitely her father's daughter, as both valiantly stood to save the American Revolution.

11

$\mathcal{I}$n *Paradise Lost,*
Females Obey:
Remembering the
Temptress Eve

Throughout hundreds of years, many women have accepted their poisoned stations in life. The men who construed their values believed females were meant to comply with a man's stern choices for them. That thinking ran deep for centuries, among even the best of bright-minded males.

True to historic references, John Milton, who wrote *Paradise Lost* and savored Christian biblical thinking, wrote the entirety of his masterpiece between 1608 and 1674. His book is still taught today in college level courses, perpetuating much of the insidious thinking that continued to hold women as inferiors. Without the opportunity to discover a way out of the demeaning, painful circumstances they had been born to, many women simply consented to their station in life. Men were simply superior to women, and that was recognized as an inarguable fact.

Milton, although an acknowledged genius, teaches within this fine piece of literature that "females are inferior to men, essentially evil, and must obey their husbands."

Worse yet, in his reference to the scriptural Adam and Eve,

Milton wrote that most certainly it was Eve who had sinned when she willfully picked the apple and shared it with Adam. The consequence of that action was that both Eve and Adam became the original sinners.

Then it is written that wickedness, by way of Eve, entered the Garden of Eden. No outside inferences today suggest that Eve was not the culprit; in fact, John Milton's argument holds that she was the tempting sinner who caused Adam's downfall.

The author's work today remains provocative in the scriptural sense. With little doubt, such thinking allows some men to continue to enjoy the harsh control of "their" women.

When pondering the control men have had over women for hundreds of years, one must accept that required submissive behavior has led to the static inferiority of women in the United States and definitely around the globe. Of course, women seldom fought back because "the Bible tells them so." Today, religious groups across the globe prevent girls and women from traveling without a male, attending schools, or working outside the home.

Realistically, few women would have had the opportunity to read *Paradise Lost*. However, there is no doubt they were kept at home and in "their place" because of a variety of religious dictums controlling women's behaviors.

Worse still, John Milton's detrimental criticism of women seemed to have accelerated the long-existing belief that females were born to be inferior to males. Women themselves seemed to simply accept their assigned menial roles. After all, young females were kept at home to learn domestic skills in hopes of becoming a wife and mother.

By the 1800s, some of this had begun to change. Selectively, women themselves began to write about that disturbing treatment. How could they have recognized or voiced the negative influence men had on their lives centuries before? Most likely some recognized it before then but knew it was best to hold their tongues. Also, books had become more available, which encouraged women writers to boldly record the truth by putting their pens to paper. Indeed, talented women were anxious to write, while others were anxious to sneak a look at books they knew they could be condemned for reading.

Ultimately, some books included truisms of the day. According to Jane Austen, "It is in truth acknowledged, that a single man in possession of a good fortune, must be in want of a wife." Austen was a superb writer and a clear-thinking woman. During her time at home in England, she had little interest in stepping into a marriage. Why, wouldn't it be better to stay with her sisters and those who loved her, where she could be freely known and accepted as a writer? After all, as a writer she meant to stretch mistaken boundaries for women and men as well.

Then a few more female writers began to surface. They started to become known and even acknowledged by their real names.

By 1869, Jane Austen had become a well-known, highly successful writer, both in England and in other countries. Many lessons within her books addressed complicated social circumstances, which eventually had her readers breaking into smiles.

England's upper-class ladies had more opportunities to read than did other women, and change was in the making when it came to matchmaking and a family's need to find appropriate husbands for their daughters.

Then, as individual women countered the historic dogmas stifling them, they began to have faith in their own possibilities. In fact, some of them commenced standing up to the minds of men who had forever thought of them as mere servants.

Well-known female writers simply knew that writing was to be their life's voice. They wrote and were read, and their books became well known. Then the money came, when eventually women authors wrote best sellers.

Could it be that *Paradise Lost*, nearly forgotten, is collecting dust in libraries?

12

*K*ate Chopin Knew Having Her Book Meant Hiding It

*T*he *Awakening*, a book by Kate Chopin, revealed things women perhaps thought but never popularly accepted, discussed, or spoke of in polite company. Published in 1899, Chopin's book walks the reader through the struggle of her female character who wants more than marriage and motherhood—hardly a popular theme in Chopin's time!

However, the book seemed to covertly open many women's minds. The true number of women who thought as Chopin did then is not certain. In fact, those who read *The Awakening* most likely hid it somewhere so they could keep their interest in the alluring subject private without ever having to explain why they had such a repugnant book.

Awakening's risk-taking main character, Edna Pontellier, has been vacationing with her two young sons on Grand Isle, a Louisiana resort on a barrier island off the coast of the Gulf of Mexico. Her husband, a New Orleans businessman, provides his family with this fashionable resort vacation. By most standards, the Pontelliers have social advantages others must have dreamt of at the time.

Chopin opens her character's thoughts to excitement beyond upscale vacations, home, and family. Edna wants more than the aristocratic Louisiana place to summer. When her boys later go to visit their grandmother and Edna returns to New Orleans, she explores the idea of sex outside of marriage. After all, her businessman husband is busy with work in New York. So she explores her fantasized personal subject. This is an opportunity born of dreams to escape from the highly structured life she lives in New Orleans. She goes forward to explore her sexual possibilities, in hopes of participating in an affair with a stranger.

Judging whether or not her life with her husband has become dull, or perhaps tedious, Edna wants to liberate herself from the trying restraints of her husband and children. At the turn of the century, a woman of acceptable character would never have taken such a conjugal risk. Somewhat naive in her understanding of such temptation, Edna has convinced herself to participate in a sexual affair.

Throughout *The Awakening*, the reader cannot help but wonder what will become of Edna Pontellier. She appears to be exploring the possibility of sex with someone besides her husband without touching the multiple pitfalls of her circumstances at a time when going headlong with her desire most likely could destroy her. Impulsively, she finds a guy who entices her. However, he runs off when it comes to becoming involved with a married woman.

Sexual behavior in the late 1800s was not even an acceptable topic. A wife was definitely supposed to provide for the needs of her husband, as well as always being there for him and their children. A couple's sex life was most often a relationship demanded by husbands and accepted by women. Sex was often an obligation for females within a marriage.

Edna finds a younger man who she believes will provide romance as well as a secret sexual relationship. Unthinkingly, she somehow believes this will provide her with a bit of independence. When she finds herself comfortably free in a rented cottage, she learns the stranger she has counted on for such excitement, instead flees from her sexual offer.

Actually those in her familiar societal circumstances would have betrayed her for violating her marriage vows or divorcing. That alone would have caused her to accept only lesser men as possible lovers. In the nineteenth century, Edna would have been seen by those in her social class as used goods.

At that time, a divorce would tarnish a woman's future more than it would that of a divorced man. Left with sexual desire and nearly ostracized by the New Orleans social community, Edna wrestles with herself.

Had she not been extremely naive she could have recognized the depths of depression that awaited her. In a small way, she did offer other women hope for changing what was considered acceptable behavior. Yet smothering herself in romantic notions, she merely alienated herself from those with acceptable social behaviors.

Feminism has come a long way from the biblical concepts. Women have gone from accepting male domination to liberating themselves by transforming society's views of acceptable roles for females in the twenty-first century.

In many ways the character, Edna, as well as the author, Kate Chopin, would be stunned by the distance feminism has traveled. Authors now often break boundaries intending to attract reading audiences and induce in them assurance that change is coming.

Edna must have stonewalled some readers with her dramatic ending. Unable to find a relationship due to her never officially ended marriage, as well as her now less than stellar reputation, Edna fails.

What reader could not remember that she walks into the coastal sea and commits suicide? Such a desperate choice is preserved on the New York City library walk: "The bird that would soar above the level plain of tradition and prejudice must have strong wings." Obviously, Edna lacked the strength to succeed at what she believed could make her happy. To be fair, in the 1800s, women's liberation, or the feminist movement, was still years in the future. That failing history for women went on and on, but today a female's success depends most often on the individual woman's choice.

Kate Chopin, the writer, married her husband when she was twenty-one years old. By the age of twenty-eight, she was the mother of six children. Her husband died and left her with huge debts, but she stepped forward, using her talent. Perhaps expected, the subject matter of *The Awakening* brought Kate Chopin some bad press. Withstanding that criticism, she continued, and her work was later acknowledged as one of the first feminist books. Over time, it has become a monumental piece of women's literature. Unfortunately, Chopin was simply ahead of her time.

So it was that in the United States readers quivered at her book's honesty about children, sex, marriage, and the well-defined limits on females. Kate Chopin and other female authors risked failure and deep criticism as they stepped out to show that women had voices that must be heard. In so doing, without thinking about their place in history, such authors made written contributions that prevailed and pushed them to believe in themselves.

Years later, singer Helen Reddy wrote the lyrics for "I Am Woman," accompanied by the music of Ray Burton. Popular in the 1980s, the song's hook says it all: "I am woman. Hear me roar." The lyrics include phrases like "wisdom born of pain" and "I am invincible." Written by Burton (the music) and Helen Reddy (the lyrics), "I Am Woman" topped the music charts, and in 1972 it was number one on the Billboard Hot 100. The powerful words that fill each stanza sustain the song of thunderous female support as part of that chorus sings out, "I am strong. I am invincible. I am woman."

Think how one thing led to another for years throughout history until women began to realize their value beyond the conventional code of marriage and motherhood.

Chopin relayed her own confinement in marriage within her nearly inconceivable book. The idea that any female would discuss her need for romance and intimacy outside of marriage had been verboten. The author's strength not only carried her forward as a writer but also helped her see her own private future ahead. That did not come easily but because she labored at it.

Apparently tough by nature, Kate Chopin carried on when her husband died, leaving her with inexplicably huge debts. Bravely, she never backed away from a financial obligation to his business failure until she could not meet the needs of her children. At that point, she moved to Saint Louis, Missouri, where her mother resided. In reality, for Chopin there was no walking into the ocean as her character had done. Instead, typical of her resilience, she thought before she acted.

She returned to her writing again. Using her talent, she resurrected feminist themes from the cellar. Some even thought of her as a near genius. In fact, Kate Chopin's own strength led her to become one of the most popular writers of her day, and she was certainly recognized by her readers as a perceptive, talented writer who was willing to lead women out of their once-accepted darkness while warning them to think before they acted against the customs of the time.

Kate Chopin put aside tears after her husband died in order to consider how she might be capable of saving her husband's failed business, but she knew only her strong personal talent could save her. In addition, that strength allowed her to believe in her ability to write and in the depth of her exploration of subject matter that would lay the groundwork for extending opportunities for tough females like herself. Even with all of those children and having lost her means of financial security, she started again as a writer. After all, as a writer, she had more to say.

Importantly, as Edna moved forward, there were still few women who would openly admit to thinking as she did. However, the author put forth a mighty roar that eventually allowed today's many satisfied, accomplished women to become independent and make their own personal choices.

How difficult is it to go against the status quo in order to succeed? Such special people change the world while leaning heavily on their own achievements. Of course there is no question that such women are exceptionally tough. They are often lonely and alone, but they are women looking ahead. Although unusual, they seldom see themselves that way. History takes care of that by ultimately remembering them for their gifts.

13

The Punishing Rest Cure When Only Men Were Physicians

How many years has it taken for men to believe that women are *not* born inferior? In most cases, hundreds, if not thousands of years, with exceptions of course.

"The Yellow Wallpaper," written by Charlotte Perkins Gilman in 1899, both shocked and eventually shattered many of the prevailing beliefs that women were men's inferiors. However, global thinking about women often still perceives women as inferior to men. Where such reasoning lingers, women are often encouraged to think they are lovingly protected when instead they are limited by being kept at home by their husbands or other male family members. Whenever or wherever male thinking decides the proper protocols for women, there remains a course of slavery for women.

Beginning in the 1800s in the United States, the much-followed American neurologist Dr. Silas Weir Mitchell gave birth to the rest cure. Whether society believed his solution for hysterical women was terrific or terrible took some years to decipher.

When Charlotte Perkins Gilman, the eventual author of "The Yellow Wallpaper," faced postpartum depression after the birth of her first child, things changed. The treatment she faced can now be defined as repulsive—a treatment endured by a talented, intelligent woman who, indeed, was even married to a physician. Unfortunately, like other physicians, her husband believed in Weir Mitchell's rest cure.

Ultimately, it was Gilman who was set back in terms of mental health because of Dr. Mitchell's inappropriate but recognized postpartum mental cure. Once on her own, she spelled out these circumstances in her semifictional short story "The Yellow Wallpaper."

Forlorn after having received the medical treatment she experienced, she went on to support the capabilities of women. At that time, women were regularly lumped together as hysterical and considered the weaker sex.

Who can imagine that a woman who gave birth, reared children, and stayed at home to cook and keep the home fires burning would receive only slim educational opportunities? Some became writers and artists by breaking the rules and pressing forward. Of course, they had plenty to write about!

Importantly, Charlotte Perkins Gilman conceptualized, wrote, and created the story that wiped out the rest cure. Until this cure was finally deemed bogus, it's likely that many women who innocently gave into the abhorrent cure suffered the true depths of insanity it induced.

By no coincidence, the story's fictional woman is imprisoned in a lovely, empty, old mansion where she is sent to become isolated in its nursery. Then matters get worse when her diary is discovered by her husband. Obviously, she had not yielded to her husband's wishes.

No doubt Gilman's voice as a writer must have upended this fraud within the mental health community of the late 1800s, replacing it with truth. Perhaps only a woman could confront the ignorance of those highly recommended psychiatrists and finally change the unfulfilling outcomes of their treatments! Eventually postpartum depression was acknowledged and treated humanely. However, women are still seen as inferiors in many places across the globe.

Looking back at the health care community of the United States in the 1800s, we find that male supremacy clearly dominated medicine and uncover a certain conceit in males themselves. Then things moved quickly, as writer Gilman suffered draconian medical treatment. In fact, "The Yellow Wallpaper" exposed both husbands and doctors, who ignorantly took the wrong path with women's mental health.

Move forward a few hundred years, and we see a much different system; health care in the United States is constantly progressing. Pregnant women under a physician's care can most often look forward to the happy conclusion of childbirth. After all, any man must wonder whether he could be brave enough to consent to such pain.

Gilman's historic story describes a birth mother who loses her sanity. And who wouldn't have gone mad in the character's situation—without accessible friends, outings, paintbrushes, books, or hope? Instead, the character's quivering mind slips into true madness. Locked up and alone, the woman has been forced into indisputable insanity.

Her madness concludes in her tearing the yellow paper from the walls of her prison with the hope of rescuing her imagined female companion who escaped by hiding there. Who could miss that Dr. Silas Weir Mitchell's professed cure had made his patient totally insane? His care should have been recognized as heartless and inhuman, but that was then and this is now.

To complete the tormented woman's mission, Gilman's main character strips off pieces of the wallpaper in order to reach the fictionalized imprisoned woman. Deservingly, her husband faints when he enters her prison to find his wife creeping around this nursery.

Charlotte Perkins Gilman risked her own reputation when she eventually wrote "The Yellow Wallpaper." By exposing the past mental health mistakes, she put physicians and husbands on a course of change. Without Gilman's story, could Americans still be following the paths of Third World countries? Instead, she crossed medical lines with her theories and saved females from medical tyranny.

The success of Gilman's short story far outlived her; it remains readily available to readers today. Instead of feeling ashamed of her postpartum despair, Gilman used her writing talent and gave the gift of her knowledge to the world. Now much of the world seems to understand that most recovering mothers need a prescribed regimen of sunshine, sleep, exercise, and quality time.

Looking back, it is fair to say that it took a woman to point out the inadequacies of Weir Mitchell's own mind. No man had stepped forward to raise suspicion about his fraudulent cures.

Charlotte Perkins Gilman attacked mental illness at a time when the subject matter was only whispered about. Significantly, she had the most to lose, since she herself had dealt with mental illness. Just how many women at that time would have been willing to bravely expose their battle with postpartum depression, especially given that hers had sent her into temporary insanity?

This is an example of the forceful power of a talented writer giving a gift to the world. Gilman worked quietly and alone. She questioned whether readers would accept her literary product. But never gave up on her illuminating piece of literature. She must have agonizingly written and rewritten until she was ready to present her story to the world.

All writers must spend hours alone working. However, in Gilman's case, her depressive aloneness was the cause, not the cure. Fortunately for other women in her situation, she exposed the truth about the insane rest cure, popular at the time so that physicians (usually males) could digest the utter failure of this treatment so mind-bogglingly called a cure.

Given the times and all she'd endured, her ability to even think about writing this story showed the mettle behind her talent. In doing so, she exposed her own illness, and she was willing to do this in hopes of changing the bleak prognosis and misdiagnosis of the medical care she had experienced herself. In fact, she went boldly ahead in written word to unravel the depth of dark postdelivery possibilities for other mothers.

Bravery always includes risk. And in this case, Charlotte Perkins Gilman's "The Yellow Wallpaper" destroyed the rest cure recommended for postpartum depression forever—at least in the United States and other developed countries. Today, experiencing postpartum depression is no longer considered shameful and can be helped when treated by well-educated male or female physicians. Published in 1935, Charlotte Perkins Gilman's "The Yellow Wallpaper" laid the groundwork for clearing up all the errors those in the health care profession had been committing when it came to the treatment of new mothers afflicted with postpartum depression.

14

$\mathscr{D}$aring Amelia Earhart: A Life of Setting Flying Records

Amelia Earhart had excitement within and a desire to reach for the future and her next challenge, whether it be climbing trees or flying, which she became determined to do after watching an air show with her family. And her desire to fly didn't just remain a dream. Rather, it was a dream she went after. She earned a flying license in 1921, and set an altitude record for women of fourteen thousand feet in 1923.

Of course, she was an independent female who went on to develop a life and reputation that remains today. Who could miss the famous female? After all, she could not have been more popular after setting one flying record after another.

Amelia became the first female to fly solo across the Atlantic; in fact, for that dangerous feat, Earhart earned the United States' Distinguished Flying Cross.

Invited to become a visiting faculty member at Purdue University, Earhart counseled women in similar careers, while also serving as a technical adviser to the university's Department of Aeronautics.

Although nearly impossible to believe, she also supported the Equal Rights Amendment guaranteeing equal rights for women in 1923! How ahead of her time and unusual this woman was in many respects. Although her flying history made her a celebrity, it meant that her combined gifts of good looks, intelligence, and outright courage simply grew the public's fascination with her. All of these traits were simply part of her innate fiber that pushed her to go onward and upward.

Even today, reaching goals, whether in the immediate or distant future, requires a woman to rely on the honesty within herself. And itemizing such targets belongs on a private must-do list.

Of course, most people acknowledge that there are situations when, after serious thought, they save some ambitious projects for later. Counting on the possibility of unsustainable projects can mean scrapping something that clearly is no longer worth the effort. Of course, the will and determination to make an effort to change things when necessary describes the life of the famous pilot Amelia Earhart.

Along with a full life both in the air and on the ground, she continued moving toward fulfilling her huge ambitions. With her feet on the ground, Amelia fell in love and eventually married George Putnam, a member of the Putnam publishing family, in 1929. But even Amelia's decision to marry took some time. George proposed to her six times before she would accept the idea of marriage. In fact, the marriage went a distance beyond 1931 marriage customs. She required a prenuptial agreement that "guaranteed her continued independence." For many reasons, Putnam was just the right man for her, since he went on to support and publicize her flying career.

Amelia and George lived a storied life. The couple agreed to support each other's individual passions and accepted the publicity that kept them in the limelight and busy. George even agreed with Amelia's determination to be the first woman to fly around the world.

By then a well-known celebrity, she challenged herself again. After all, Earhart had become the first woman to fly solo nonstop from coast to coast, while setting a new transcontinental speed record for flying. For this prestigious flight, President Herbert Hoover honored her with the Distinguished Flying Cross, while National Geographic presented Amelia with a gold medal. Importantly then and now, no one has ever doubted her fearless nature, her exciting, just-do-it goals, and her stunningly attractive good looks that both women and men acknowledged!

Her early exit from life on that well-planned around-the-world flight made her immortal in a way few women have ever become.

When she chose Fred Noonan as her navigator, she knew just what she was doing. Still something went wrong.

Amelia Earhart and her navigator disappeared on June 2, 1937, over the Central Pacific Ocean near Howland Island, where it is believed she and Noonan ran out of fuel. The US Coast Guard cutter *Itasca* had sporadic radio contact with her as she approached Howland Island and believed she would have ditched her Lockheed aircraft in the ocean. Though the pair was never found, they were often looked for. Newer theories suggest that both Amelia and Fred Noonan may have made it to Gardner Island but eventually died there.

When history points to this one-of-a-kind feat with an unknown ending, Amelia Earhart and her missing Lockheed plane still stirs interest. Her success as a female flyer, her zest for life, and her pluck remain an example today for other women. As they celebrate Amelia's life and accomplishments, they are perhaps inspired to go forward with their own unbelievable plans.

Amelia's early yearning to fly quickly became a commitment she would maintain throughout her life. She never strayed from her plans to fly. Her devotion to the world of aviation is in itself an example of sheer determination. Then too, regardless of the twists and turns along her path, she bonded herself to her dangerous objectives. The best-known adventurous female of her time, Amelia pressed unflinchingly forward to get where she wanted to be.

Looking back on failed opportunities was not her way. Of course, she allowed for temporary disappointment, but her enthusiasm for flying remained ardent. Evidently her ambition overrode any fears she might have had. No one doubted that Amelia was self-reliant.

Known as a "daring darling," Amelia had the vivacity to look ahead. And of course her intelligence allowed her to sift through life's choices while continuing to thrive and advance her aviation goals.

Who wouldn't believe that such an unconventional woman

would risk live and limb, financial security, and criticism in order to participate in an uncharted future? That was Amelia's core value. That was Amelia.

One's degree of courage is most often born to the self-assured. Still, to follow a career that requires resolute bravery, one must have an internal fortitude that speaks to her soul and be willing to listen. In Amelia Earhart's lifetime, she became famous for forwarding flight. She not only talked about it, she set out to live it. And what an example she was for other women!

Fearless Earhart lived her dreams. She also influenced other clever females to pilot their own dreams. Then she was gone! Certainly she was never forgotten.

She died somewhere in the Pacific, along with her copilot. Neither Earhart nor Fred Noonan sent any clues that ever played out. And although messages had been received along the flight, they suddenly stopped.

Although she died differently than many women or men, Amelia Earhart's life was of value to the world. Her successes were in their time and remain today breathtaking.

The legacy she left behind for each female pilot remains: Go after it all. What could be better for Amelia Earhart's legacy than knowing she contributed to other female pilots' successes? Perhaps she assumed that beyond her aeronautical time, other females would set records beyond the pale, where more universes waited to be visited. It's no surprise that today explorers have set their sights on thousands of known planets far beyond our earth, anxious to set spacecrafts down on these distant lands. Or, possibly, visitors from those planets will set their own crafts down right here.

What Amelia Earhart started is still many adventures beyond us. Deep thinkers know that another female here on earth or living on a distant plant will be bold, tough, vivacious, and self-reliant!

15

Danica Patrick, Fast Track Driver: "Be the Best, Not the Best Girl"

The theme Danica Patrick uses when speaking to female audiences says so much about who she is and continues to be. "Be the best, not the best girl," she tells the women she speaks with. That describes her path in both INDYCAR racing and now NASCAR racing, which she's followed since she left school at sixteen years old and got a GED, after which she went to England to participate in Kart racing. While there, she also raced the Formula Ford.

Who could mistake her ambition and dedication? She has made her intent clear—to propel herself toward a successful racing dream come true.

With spunk (along with the early support of her parents), Danica has continued to be successful in open-wheel racing! While in the past some men may have labeled her one of the weaker sex and even many females may have believed she should be home in the kitchen, fortunately much of that thinking has changed. Women like Danica Patrick have proven themselves to be successful at fulfilling their dreams. She has raced forward and broken from the male perception that women aren't drivers, seen instead as a triumphant woman.

There's no question about it. Danica's strength and love for what she does sets her apart. And she owns her public image. However, all of her success depends on her devotion to auto racing.

Patrick's history is a succession of successes. She won the Indy Japan 300 in 2008, gaining the "only women's victory in an INDYCAR Series race" and later placed third in the 2009 Indianapolis 500, with the "highest finish there ever by a woman." From INDY racing, she went on to race in the NASCAR Nationwide Series and also to the NASCAR Sprint Cup Series. In 2013, she became the first female in the NASCAR Sprint Cup Series pole position. In fact, she turned in the fastest qualifying lap since 1990. And this position qualified her for the Daytona 500.

Separately and awesomely, Danica Patrick earned eighth place in the 2013 Daytona race—the highest ever finish for a woman.

Patrick's parents fully support her life's dream; both her father and mother work for her. After all, they are needed, since she has a terrific website, a bus to be driven, and a business enterprise to be managed.

Danica, beautiful on and off the track, has led a near perfect life, which many women believe would include a husband. And she did try marriage.

In 2005, she married her physical therapist, Paul Edward Hospenthal. However after seven years, the couple agreed to an amicable divorce in 2012. With all those road trips, races, and practices, it was easy to guess that married life could be difficult. But Patrick may one day be tempted to marry again. In any case, according to track news, for a while, "she was dating" driver Ricky Stenhouse Jr.

However, a close examination of Danica's success and devotion to racing makes it clear that her life's wish as a young girl was not romance. As a young woman, Danica did not even go to a high school prom. As most celebrities know, marriages seldom seem to boost career choices. And today well-known females and males alike have to make serious choices about how they choose to live their lives. Highly successful women and men today have to cautiously ask themselves who they are and where they hope their lives may take them. After all, it's clear that Danica Patrick is a driver working to win a race and not depending on her beauty to put her across that finish line.

Patrick's mind thrives on racetracks and winning. Simply put, NASCAR'S Danica Patrick belongs to the world of that high-speed circular competition that defines her ambition. Add to that, she has a photographic memory, and it's plain to see that her days are filled with demanding plans and practices that consume both her mind and body.

This woman who is addicted to speed is a shrewd, tough cookie behind the wheel of her number 10 race car, which she handles like a piece of dynamite. Thrilled to be behind the car's wheel and determined to control its winning destiny, Patrick is keenly aware this fast-moving object can be either her best pal or her worst nightmare.

Being known has its ups and downs, but that isn't what she thinks about as her courage takes her around a track, following a well-designed plan to get out front.

To the world that knows her, Patrick is not simply another woman making cupcakes or putting her children on a school bus. She is a committed driver pursuing the sport she loves.

Who would ever argue that Danica isn't her own woman when taking into consideration the choices she has made and the things she has given up since she left high school to become who she wanted to be?

And who would argue that she doesn't know her math, logic, and basic engineering? There are plenty of lives to live, but no woman should merely be classified by gender.

Each female (or male) has choices. Most often, they are born with the traits that lead them to success. People like Danica Patrick have certainly listened to their own voices for years, prompting them to stay with the plan and not be deterred. That attribute came to her early. A good-looking woman in a man's world, who never fears being different—that is who she worked to become, and it's who she is.

Patrick made a professional plan that would help her to excel as a race car driver—definitely not thinking about being a noted female driver. The possibility of failure must have never entered her mind, although she must consider the risk of being seriously injured (or killed) for moments prior to a race or upon finishing one. Such unspoken thoughts are the business Danica chose to marry. Importantly, she is exactly where she wants to be, and that's why she remains a daring world-class driver.

Nothing is so fantastic that dreams fall from the sky into anyone's lap. The simple truth is that an uplifting optimism is a must in every sport. What stamina and faith Danica has in herself. With track racing as the life she chose, can there be any question that her attitude and willpower will triumph?

Winning at sports never comes easy. It takes continued strength of mind, body, and talent to triumphantly win! In between successes, a driver has to have some grit in order to return to the track believing another victory lies ahead.

16

*F*irst African American Woman Elected to the US Congress

B right and ambitious, Shirley Chisholm made it happen. She became the first African American woman in the United States Congress. But how did she do it?

In 1968, Chisholm was elected to represent New York State in the United States House of Representatives. The perky young woman, at forty years old, was so well liked that she ended up serving seven terms in Congress.

Earlier in her life, Chisholm moved to Barbados with her grandmother, but she returned to the United States to attend a teachers college, followed by Brooklyn College and then Columbia University. In 1975, she received an Honorary Doctor of Law degree.

Favorably, she spoke often about the 1960s and how women began to see changes for themselves in America. "Being female and black were expected obstacles for me," she said. "Yet being a female put more obstacles in my path than being black."

Chisholm's honesty gathered many supportive women around her. And to put it straight to the public, she added, "There is little place in the political scheme of things for a creative personality, for a fighter. Anyone who takes that role must pay the price."

Lovely and looking more like a model than a political champion, Chisholm never shied away from what she saw as the truth. A favorite topic she spoke often about at the time was women's liberation. Her thinking, in combination with her courage to speak out under those unique circumstances, said it all.

A favorite saying of the African American Chisholm was, "The emotional, sexual, and psychological stereotyping of females begins when the doctor says, 'It's a girl.'" No one could have better explained the inequities females experienced.

And Chisholm had a lasting affect on her constituents in New York and across the entirety of the United States.

When Congressman Chisholm and her sisters were youngsters, they left her parents' home to be with their grandmother in Barbados. Of course no complaints there. Instead, Shirley Chisholm remembered the importance of the traditional British-style education provided her while she was living there.

Women today should remember that schoolteachers were some of the first women in the United States to have jobs. Chisholm followed that pattern upon returning to the United States. She gladly accepted an offer that would mean income for her. Very few professional jobs of any kind were available to women at the time.

However, once elected to Congress, Shirley fearlessly pressed forward with her political agenda. She endorsed key issues related to educational opportunities, racial equality, and the empowerment of women. She even made a bid for president of the United States in order to push her message. Although she didn't win the election, she was pleased with the journey, and she won more delegates than her backers ever would have expected.

During her life she married, divorced, and married again. And although she moved to Florida and was nominated to become the US Ambassador to Jamaica, she had to refuse the honor because of her declining health. By the time she moved to Florida, she had begun suffering from bad health and had several strokes. And as no surprise to her, she experienced threats and brushes with death, including three assassination attempts while she was a public figure. What else could have been expected at this time? Just speaking out against the right thing can still get a person killed.

Her character traits were a perfect equation. Shirley Chisholm smiled a lot while pushing her often-disliked agendas. This was a woman who stood strong when she knew many others hoped she would fail.

Regardless, she kept that smile on her face while pushing forward with her dynamic personality. Her stay in Barbados prepared her for life in the United States. She quickly assimilated both countries into her life's direction. Shirley Chisholm was a go-getter, as well as a pointedly humorous woman. She chose the right words when hoping to influence an audience and garner support for her forward thinking.

Congresswoman Shirley Chisholm meant to encourage exceptionalism and carefully reminded her many audiences, "You don't make progress by standing on the sidelines, whimpering, and complaining. You make progress with ideas."

Always bolstering her own beliefs, Chisholm was an intelligent woman who knew how to go after issues that would make things better for people in America who needed her on their side.

Congresswoman Chisholm was a fighter with a smile!

17

Zora Neale Hurston Forever!
Their Eyes Were Watching God

As a child in the early 1900s, Zora Neale lived in the isolated town of Eatonville, right at the edge of the Florida Everglades. As a developing thinker, she already had her mind on something beyond the swampland around her. When her mother died and her father married again, she moved on beyond those limited boundaries. Yet the town of her childhood was unique enough in its own right to give her courage.

Eatonville was known then as the only independently chartered African American settlement in Florida. Reaching around the town's boundaries were both the swampland's isolation and Eatonville's isolated history. Eatonville's water, fauna, and native wildlife invited thinking. No question, the great swamp could provoke thoughts of both heaven and hell, and the sharp-minded Hurston accumulated a little of both over time. After all, Zora had a lot to learn along the way, as many people do.

However, as a young woman, she reached beyond her present circumstances, looked beyond them, stood on her own, made mistakes, and focused her mind on long-term possibilities. Like many women, Hurston learned to hold close those memories of where she had been and the vision of where she wanted to go. Zora Hurston's mind could switch quickly from "do it" to "don't do it." Frightfully this behavior, on occasion, turned to bad judgment that could have ended her success, as well as her life.

Hurston's lifeline included more than one husband, whom she ultimately divorced. Beginning to understand that she had some real potential provided both pluses and minuses.

Zora understood her individual victories would require ambition, which also meant leaving others behind when she found something better waiting. Of course, who could accept Zora using them until she found something better? She had a tendency to take off while leaving relatives or suitors or even husbands behind.

At any rate, her intelligence and independence could conflict with her life. To most men, she was a threat. Simply put, Zora was often a threat to most men's perceived masculinity. Times were changing a bit in the United States, and she liked the progress she had made. Still, in the early 1900s, a huge number of women were surely married to men who expected to have the final say.

Her book *Their Eyes Were Watching God* turns on such shifting thoughts. Hurston bravely went forward to write fictional pieces about men and their treatment of women. She had experienced male domination and had often run to escape it. As a developing writer, she ensured the mistreatment of females found a way into her successful books.

Significantly, Hurston was the child of two former slaves, which had to have compelled her to crash through barriers that might lead her to achieve her goals. In time, she did just that. Zora Neale earned an associate's degree from Howard University, was awarded a bachelor's of arts from Barnard College, and studied anthropology at Columbia University.

Importantly, too, she was involved with other artists within the Harlem Renaissance. During the 1920s, this group of talented men and women lived and worked in Harlem, New York City, and were acknowledged worldwide as the center of the New Negro Movement.

She wrote and joined others there who were beginning to be valued in both the United States and Europe. Other talented individuals there included writer Langston Hughes, singer Billie Holiday, and musician Louis Armstrong. This group also touched on the impetus for social change in America.

Hurston fit in right away. Importantly, though, her early books often acknowledged the inferior circumstances of women of all races.

Today her acclaimed books, still widely read, open eyes to the deep necessity for change. Hurston's readers value her spunk, as well as her vibrant storytelling. Hurston's *Their Eyes Were Watching God* is frequently selected for university studies or suggested to readers by friends.

Zora Neale Hurston's talent exploded into reality with *Their Eyes Were Watching God*; both her prose and her storytelling skills shone. She knew her ability would be recognized eventually, as long as she never gave up along the way. Today, this book remains one of the best in the English language because it contains the ideas Hurston believed in. She puts outsiders in her shoes and allows them to think along with her. Hurston's writing held to a theme that was clearly a question in her own life: Why should women rely entirely on a man?

Although Hurston wanted to be recognized for her talents and abilities, she never lived to witness those dreamed of likelihoods. Instead women then would continue to live and be controlled in a man's world for years to come. Still Zora must have believed in those possibilities, or she wouldn't have exposed the facts that would ultimately change things.

The traits that made up Hurston's personality took her beyond boundaries set for females. She set an accelerated pace for herself and for other females to consider trying.

Linked to this was her tenacious desire to express herself, to leave behind that which would hold her back, and to discover opportunities to learn more. *Mediocre* was never a word she found acceptable along her journey. How pleased she would be to know that she still brings life to literature in a most needed way.

Her strongest trait was herself. She never accepted defeat, instead holding tightly to the belief that women would ultimately be able to participate in nearly anything that men had been able to freely do from birth.

Hurston wrote about change and acted openly on the likelihood that the change she hoped for would come to fruition. Then, too, somewhere there was a semblance of God beyond her physical reach that had convinced her she was right. She wanted others to share that faith in order that they too might realize a better future.

Zora Neale Hurston never quit. Her staying power has been a gift to the multitude of women who have benefited by following in her footsteps.

18

*O*prah's Talent Buried Trauma: When Dad and Nashville Saved Her

Oprah Winfrey eventually became known worldwide as simply Oprah. She became the woman the world now knows her as despite her early childhood, which no one would envy. She had a frightful young life that most likely would have destroyed others, but she escaped. It is essential to know what enabled her to survive in order to become the world's Oprah.

Starting out, she pleased audiences with her smile and her personal interaction with them. Soon the popularity grew, and she was recognized as preeminent in many radio, television, and screen categories.

Born the only child of unwed parents who quickly went their separate ways, the young Oprah innately had a lot going for her. She was a precocious child, who knew how to push mountains aside while keeping a beautiful smile on her face. Obviously, her multiple talents grew as she grew. And the young Winfrey's dreams unquestionably built in time to contribute to her celebrity.

While at home with her grandmother (her mother worked during the day) young Oprah received important guidance. Her grandmother taught her to read, and by two and a half years old, this bright girl with the warm smile was able to skip kindergarten and enter the third grade.

Then things changed. Winfrey went to live with her father in Nashville, Tennessee. Life with him saved her. He was both aware of her ability and willing to give her some dedicated time, guidance, and structure, even though he was a busy man with a business of his own. Even moving around a bit, Oprah knew she had been fortunate to see these new possibilities.

Although still young at the time, she must have gleaned that moving to her father's home made her a fortunate girl. The bright Oprah must have worried, however, about how long she would be able to live in Nashville with her father.

Sure enough, Oprah's mother wanted her daughter to leave her father's home and return to live with her in Mississippi. One might guess there was a struggle going on within Oprah about this sudden change that would take her away from her dad.

Unfortunately, once back in Mississippi, young Oprah faced a number of spot-on nightmares, which were terribly real and horrific. While her mother worked outside of the home, trusted male family members sexually abused the young girl repeatedly.

Looking back at these disturbing circumstances tells us a lot about the child Oprah was and the woman she would become. Oprah was clever. She knew she had to contact her dad about returning to live with him. He agreed, and she took off to Nashville, where he was not only pleased to have her back but also quickly realized he had saved his daughter's life.

Subsequently, her father set out to erase the turmoil she had endured, making sure she would be able to go forward with her life. Oprah never forgot that it was her father who increased her chances of a successful life. Apparently, the move to Nashville was the matrix for her up-and-coming celebrity.

Back in her father's home, Oprah was expected to read books and follow his rules. What a change! She found with him a structure she was expected to accept. Oprah would later say the environment she experienced while living with her father "turned my life around." In addition to reading, she was to write reports on the books she read as well as learning new words. Obviously her father was strict because he loved and wanted her to have serious goals.

Some adolescents would resist such demands, but she didn't! No wonder that when Oprah became a star, she started the popular Oprah's Book Club. No doubt she was hoping that people of all ages and genders would share a bit of what her father had taught her to appreciate.

While still in Nashville, Winfrey began college at Tennessee State University. There, she continued to achieve, by winning titles such as Miss Black Nashville and Miss Tennessee State, both in her freshman year. However, she didn't finish her education at that point in time. Oprah had gotten a taste of stardom and chose to leave college behind.

Who could have missed her beautiful smile and perfect voice? It wasn't long before she launched the highly acclaimed *Oprah Winfrey Show*, which to no surprise appealed to most of the human race.

In 1987, Tennessee State University invited her to speak at the school's commencement. By then Oprah seemed to have been acknowledged everywhere. Although Oprah was nationally syndicated, she'd never completed a small piece of her coursework at the university in Nashville. And of course, she could hear her father's voice telling her a college degree was essential.

With that voice in her head, she decided to complete her work before she accepted the invitation to speak to the students graduating from Tennessee State. How could she accept this honor when those she would be speaking to had completed their degrees and she had not? Even though she was now a film star and had founded her company, Harpo Productions, she knew what she had to do. She had to complete that degree at Tennessee State she'd started years earlier.

When she fulfilled the requirements and earned her degree, Winfrey made her way to Nashville to the commencement ceremonies. She would speak to her audience not just as the recognizable Oprah Winfrey, but also as a graduate of the university.

Oprah never went looking for a husband to provide her with

security. She simply didn't need to. However, she does have a private life and has lived happily with a man for many years.

The hardships of her childhood did not steal her successful future from her. For Oprah Winfrey, like so many females, was as tough as steel. And she was and is as loved as any woman could be by her huge following.

In many ways, Winfrey followed her dad. His methods were somewhat hers. She became a popular figure who knew how to listen and approach people's questions in rather the same way her father had done with her. And somehow she survived and thrived in spite of those early molestations and having gone without someone she could trust until she moved into her father's home in Nashville.

Oprah was smart. Quick of mind as a young female, she acted swiftly in order to escape what her Mississippi relatives had done to her. The young, smart Oprah got on the phone and called her dad!

Accepting her father's strict discipline took some work. But her intelligence told her his home was where she belonged. She knew her father loved her and had her best in mind.

Undeniably, her talent counted, but her ambition pushed her to keep going until she was simply Oprah wherever she went. That took energy, faith, and the desire to be independent.

Oprah Winfrey's success should guide others to concede that nothing ever comes easily. She is a great icon to follow for anyone who is planning a fulfilling career. And what a lesson she has set for young people, who must learn how to make good choices!

19

Ayaan Hirsi Ali's Resolve Early to Stand Up to Radicals

Hirsi Ali up and left her home in Kenya in 1992, with the plan of becoming a citizen of the Netherlands. She wanted to escape a forced marriage to a distant relative she had been promised to but had never met.

Although Somalia was Ali's birth country, she had been a refugee in several other African countries and had thought over her planned escape to the Netherlands, where she believed she could be free to live her own life. She did not intend for this forced marriage to drag her back to the man in Somalia.

Yet upon reaching the Netherlands, she was startled to learn that radical Islam had also chosen her destination city to call home. In a fix now, she continued with her plan anyway. She provided Dutch authorities with false information in order to obtain citizenship. But the subterfuge was uncovered, which threatened both her escape from the marriage and her plan to seek asylum in her chosen European country.

Ultimately (after explaining to authorities her need to hide there), she was accepted at the University of Leiden in Amsterdam. There, she proceeded to earn her master's degree.

Ali had much to overcome in order to live the life she'd hoped to find in the Netherlands. And of course she believed no man should be allowed to own a female. Custom in some African countries allows a family to promise a female in marriage to a man she has never seen. Why would such a husband have ownership over any woman? Why would a man believe he could own a smart, ambitious woman?

Like many African women, as a girl, Hirsi Ali had suffered the custom of surgical removal of her clitoris. The implication of this kind of female mutilation is startling. The surgical procedure is intended to prevent a female's sexual desires and, indeed, keep her from wandering to other sexual partners. A man's satisfaction with his wife's body meant simply forcing himself on her. These practices are known as world health circumcisions.

Although born in Somalia, Hirsi Ali had left there in 1977 with her family to live in Saudi Arabia, Ethiopia, and Kenya. The purpose of her later escape was singular—she simply hoped to find political asylum in the Netherlands.

After she had obtained her master's degree in political science, Ali began to alert Europeans to the dangers ahead of them. Well liked there, she was elected as deputy for Amsterdam's Liberal Party. However, by 2002, Ali had switched her allegiance to the Labor Party. In fact, at that time, Ali was ahead of the world in terms of what lay in the future. She often publically explained that mistreatment of women among the Muslim community, even there in the Netherlands, was growing rapidly.

The spreading of Muslim beliefs that would trap women in subservience—regardless of where they lived or how far they had migrated in order to lead decent lives—was moving at a faster pace than ever. Fooled for certain, women who had come to escape their fates believed wholeheartedly that the Netherlands supported change for them. How unfortunately wrong they were. Instead of being liberated from Muslim control, they soon learned their dreams of liberation were not going to happen. There would be no free and open lives for them. Most of the women lost hope. Muslims in the Netherlands enslaved women, although it was never spoken of in those terms.

Discovering that they had not found a safe haven in their chosen country after all was terrifying for the independent females who had migrated there. The extremists were gathering supporters and enforcing laws even in other developed countries.

Even in America, women's liberation had become somewhat of a joke. The movement had not gone forward smoothly and had taken years to become accepted. Nevertheless, the talk of such acceptance had been batted around there with negative suggestions popping up by both men and conservative women.

Then the apocalypse hit the Netherlands. In 2004, well-known filmmaker Theo van Gogh bravely produced a film, along with the support of Hirsi Ali, about the frightening issues that women faced. For this he was shot dead by a twenty-six-year-old Dutch-born Muslim. Van Gogh was killed for stepping out publically in support of women's issues. The killer attached a note to van Gogh's body saying Ali would be killed next.

By now, these Muslim extremists seemed to have the upper hand. Killings in Paris and Belgium by extremists in 2015 showed their determination to continue their campaign and their belief that killing those who thought differently from them was working. By 2016, hundreds of innocent people were attacked and killed in Paris and Belgium.

Today, Ayaan Hirsi Ali retains her strength and continues to safeguard women's rights. She now lives in Massachusetts, writes best-selling books, and speaks at universities around the country. She is still protected, as she has been since leaving the Netherlands to live in the United States.

While in the United States, Ali met and married a Harvard professor. She lives in Massachusetts with her husband and their daughter.

Ali's strength has never wavered. And few other women have traveled as far or worked as tirelessly without caving into the customs of their birth countries.

Ayaan Hirsi Ali's path has included writing. When she moved to the United States in 2007, she continued to publish her books. Who could overlook her intelligence and fierce resolve when she published *The Caged Virgin*? Indeed this best seller remains an often-read, anti-Islamic book written by an Islamic woman.

Perhaps it must be said again that it has been Hirsi Ali's mindful resolve that has made her willing to carry on in the face of threats and the assassination of her compatriot film producer Theo van Gogh.

Strength comes in many packages. However it takes a variety of abilities to forge ahead to achieve one's goals. Ali has never slowed down or changed her support of women. And, despite the inherent risks, she has never quit writing about the complexities of women across the globe who have followed the Muslim demands to be covered from head to toe or sent to a back room like a misbehaving child, where they cannot participate in men's knowledge or decision making.

Life often gives others the opportunity to stand up for what is correct, but doing so takes courage. Certainly the world needs others like Ali who will speak out against the sexual and personal bondage of women. Of course, bravery has explicit risks. Attempting to change long-held medieval practices still compulsory in many countries, where women have few choices, is no small feat.

A person's sense of right and wrong usually comes from within, eventually coming out in the form of actions. No one should doubt that the lovely Ayaan Hirsi Ali has plenty of resolve left. Perhaps knowing of her dedicated mission will inspire other intelligent females to press forward and change ancient, terrifying practices against women.

20

*A*zar Nafisi's Postrevolution Iran: The Iranian Revolution Meant Run Now

Professor Azar Nafisi grew up in Tehran, Iran, where her father was the mayor. She loved her home and the opportunities she had there. But then suddenly, the Iranian Revolution grabbed hold of Iran. Led by the Ayatollah Khomeini, the revolution began with a sudden coup and sent Iran back to an unexpected, terrifying dark past that quickly had a stranglehold on the entire country.

Nafisi was teaching English literature at the University of Tehran at that time, although she had lived outside of Iran earlier while studying in the United States to earn her PhD at the University of Oklahoma. What a blow it was when everything suddenly changed—especially for Iranian women.

Like other women, Azar Nafisi dressed as women did in free and open countries. She had no idea that severe rules from hundreds of years past would quickly reappear within her home country.

However, Muslim law covered the entirety of Iran as quickly as the Ayatollah had announced it. Females everywhere in Iran were immediately mandated to cover their bodies in black from head to toe. Professor Nafisi was soon fired from the University of Tehran for refusing to wear the compulsory Islamic veil and clothing.

Iran's return to antiquated laws rocked the watching world. Worst of all, no input or debate went forward because the controlling religious flashback simply took hold.

To imagine the pain Nafisi suffered as a result, one must remember that the city of Tehran had been her home. She'd earned both her undergraduate degree and her master's degree at the University of Tehran. Then she'd chosen to travel to the United States to earn her PhD.

Now back home, she watched things change quickly from bad to worse. Khomeini and those standing with him pressed forward with their agenda, using their home-styled Revolutionary Guard to rid the country of those who did not think like the new religious leader. Anyone who went against the new order was executed. Many ancient religious restrictions returned, particularly penalties for females who disobeyed the Ayatollah's declarations. In fact, they were quickly arrested.

Azar must have known she too could lose her life at any time! Instead, her toughness broke loose.

By April 1, 1979, Iran officially voted by national referendum to become an Islamic Republic and to approve a new theocratic republican constitution, whereby Khomeini became the "Supreme Leader" of the country.

Remarkably, Azar Nafisi carefully selected female students who secretly joined her inside her home to read books she had selected. Once inside, the visiting students ditched their black robes and headscarves in order to relax in the modern clothes they had worn beneath the covers they were now forced to wear. Although hardly free or openly defiant in their city, in Nafisi's home, the women were free to question, to think, and to analyze the books they read. Their mentor had written some of the books and had chosen other authors for the young women to read.

The young women were thrilled to have a momentary escape from the now rigid city—to forget for a while the controlled, frightening circumstances outside Nafisi's home. Surely, they enjoyed the cloistered freedom together with their teacher.

Of the thirteen books Nafisi and her students read privately, Vladimir Nabokov's *Lolita* found its way into the title of the book Nafisi would one day write about the experience—*Reading Lolita in Iran*.

How outraged the Iranians would have been if they had known what these young women read and learned in Nafisi's home. Although Azar's book became a best seller outside of Iran, there is nothing more impressive than these young undergraduates and their teacher, who hid their literary hunger and secretly continued to pursue their thirst for knowledge. What danger each woman faced if caught in this hiding place. How terrible it is to know there are places in the world where human beings face threats for simply reaching out to learn and, conversely, where others accept being enslaved by controlling governments.

Apparently many believe that ignorance is bliss. Certainly, those who prey upon them foster such thinking.

Today Nafisi continues to write and speak out in the United States, where she now lives. She has taught at Johns Hopkins University in Baltimore while continuing to write books. Honorably, she carries her message promoting worldwide women's liberation forward.

Nafisi remains a popular speaker at gatherings where such threats to people everywhere must be addressed. Additionally, she writes and lives in Baltimore with her husband.

Professor of English literature may be Nafisi's title at Johns Hopkins, but *courage* should no doubt be included in her name.

Her toughest stand came immediately after she was first threatened in Tehran for going against the frightening changes that were rapidly running over her country. She didn't run. Instead, she wisely hid her determination to battle ignorance. And nothing has stopped her since.

Internal strength isn't necessarily something that leaps out at people. But being tough by not backing down takes unusual courage.

Every country has a history of oppressing women or attempting to control them. That's a truth that is fearful to acknowledge. But never settle on a government that wants to remove the rights of women.

Azar Nafisi came to fear her beloved country and subsequently left Iran. How courageous she and her students had been to gather secretly in Nafisi's home.

21

$\mathcal{S}$andra Day O'Connor's Upbringing: *Real* Work on Her Family Ranch

Q uite the opposite of most children, Sandra Day grew up on her family's Lazy B Ranch, where she and her brother knew what real work was, as it was expected of them at an early age. And yes, Sandra Day's demanding yet exciting upbringing was most likely why she went on to dedicate herself to accomplishment. She never chose an easy path. Genetically, she was a resilient female.

At her parents' Lazy B Ranch in Arizona, young Sandra's childhood included hard work. She branded cattle and learned to fix almost anything that was broken. And though she lived miles from the closest school, she did not miss out on education, since by four years old, she already had become a competent reader.

Her parents decided it was time for their precocious daughter to leave the ranch to live with her grandmother and attend school. Most certainly, she missed her parents at the Lazy B, but she knew a stimulating future awaited her.

In school Sandra studied and did well, and she often saw her parents. As a teen, she kept an eye on her future. Her school records convinced her to apply to a superior college—Stanford.

Sandra Day was not only accepted to California's Stanford University; she graduated summa cum laude and immediately applied to Stanford Law School. Now this could have been a problem, since few women in the United States had become lawyers in the 1950s. But Day went on to graduate from Stanford Law in 1952 as a member of the *Stanford Law Review* and holding a place among the top ten of her graduating class.

Female rejection was definitely noted at this time. In fact, Day's intellectual success was so unique it was noteworthy. Her acceptance into law school made her known, for she had broken a barrier. Across the country, men obstinately threw books on the floor of law libraries in order to shoo women away from what male students were convinced must be a man's exclusive domain. Similar types of rejection impeded women from entering many fields of employment.

Most surprising to Sandra Day O'Connor, by then married to a student of her law school graduating class, was her introduction to employment. She was taken aback by her first offer out of Stanford Law, which was truly insulting; the position was that of a legal assistant in a law office. After all, at the time, women were not supposed to compete with men.

Soon, though, Sandra's husband, John O'Connor, was drafted into the United States Army. Both husband and wife went to Germany, where John was assigned a position as an attorney in the United States Judge Advocates General Corps. Right behind him, Sandra found a spot as a civilian lawyer in the Quartermaster Corps.

Sandra Day O'Connor also took time to have three sons before she went on to be hired as an attorney. After Ronald Reagan was elected president of the United States, he nominated Sandra Day O'Connor in 1981 to the United States Supreme Court, where she was speedily confirmed. Moreover, she became the first female elected to the nation's top legal position.

By 2006, Justice O'Connor, after twenty-four years in the high court, retired from her valued position in the District of Columbia.

Seldom remembered is her breast cancer surgery in 1988 and, later in that same year, a surgery to remove her appendix. She was obviously a stalwart female her entire life. Then another loss came with her husband John's death after his bout with Alzheimer's disease.

In 2016, at eighty-six, this remarkable woman and first female on the United States Supreme Court was alive and part of her Arizona community.

For most people, the home environment in which they grew up counts for a lot. How nice it would be if others could absorb the positive lessons O'Connor gained from her childhood at the Lazy B Ranch. Still, people are seldom created to be equal at any task. Most often such influences come from genetics, environment, and always fortitude.

Without question, Sandra Day O'Connor prepared for her future and sought to achieve goals she believed would carry her forward toward her pursuits at home and as a stellar student, lawyer, and even Supreme Court Justice of the United States.

Remember, though, she married after her graduation from Stanford Law; went with her husband to Germany when he was drafted; and upon returning home, took time away from her law practice to have three children. As would be expected from such a woman, she chose to stay at home with her children while they were young. In so many words, she thought, acted on the decisions she made, and kept in mind her ultimate goal to return to her work as a lawyer. Not unexpectedly, her organizational skills boosted her effectiveness as a wife, mother, and lawyer.

Supreme Court Justice O'Connor threw her intense energy toward her goals. Her life can serve as an example for other women striving to achieve the competence and tenacity that never failed Sandra Day O'Connor. Obviously, O'Connor led, and other women followed. What a woman!

22

$\mathscr{S}$teinem Knew What Awaited: Women's Rights Must Go Forward

If the feminist movement of the 1960s and 1970s didn't have Gloria Steinem's name on it, then the Women's Rights Movement has never existed. Steinem gathered support and, at the same time, was often subjected to hate-filled attacks by her detractors. Despite these attacks, enthusiasm to grow female participation blossomed, becoming ever more forceful and better known. Throughout this fight for the liberation of women, Ms. Steinem stood behind her hopes for women, and she continues to do so today.

A courageously intelligent individual, Steinem was never a falling star as many had hoped she would be. But she was obviously a star that got under men's skin. With her help, women's intent to be liberated from beneath their fellow men grew to huge proportions.

Women of all ages in the United States were prepared to fight! They were tired of holding only the most menial jobs. They'd seen that they often were the last to be hired and the first to be fired. And it was no surprise that good looks might get a woman more points than her résumé when a man was doing the hiring.

Women had also learned that a woman's youth didn't take her

far, even if she was hired. A male boss could tire of his hire when his female employee no longer got the wows he craved from his business cronies.

No man had expected Ms. Steinem to step into the scene and awaken women, showing them how they should fight to change their situations. Seldom could men accept that Steinem had what it took to stand up against the past male legacy. For years, men had inequitably ruled the roost. Women with required eyeglasses got a desk next to the file cabinet, even when they had the best of credentials.

As Gloria Steinem became a bad name among many men and some women, she successfully published *Ms.* magazine in 1971, expecting to reach more women who wanted to learn more about their futures. Ambitious women were excited about the magazine and its text. Thrillingly, Gloria Steinem's project for women pressed forward.

There were jokes about *Ms.* regardless of the publication's popularity. Looking back, you can find other women who had worked to build women's movements earlier but had failed or had simply lacked the backing Gloria was able to develop.

In fact, ensuring opportunities for women is a challenge much of the world may never accept. In some countries, a woman can be punished for so much as expressing a thought about shaking the status quo, and retaliation can be harsh and severe, including even death by stoning.

Women supporting Steinem sought equality in paychecks, bright opportunities for leadership, and the ability to keep pressing forward and demanding change.

Fortunately, a growing number of women refused to be discouraged. Yet this, too, must be remembered: Many women continued to stand behind their men or simply were unwilling to believe in their own abilities.

Weighing people's abilities is necessary. In limited ways, many people's skills are valued financially, while others' skills may never provide a large paycheck. For example, total equality for all under the law does not mean that every man will play in the National Basketball

Association or every woman will become an Olympic swimmer. And of course Steinem did not set out to argue such nonsense.

Fearlessly, Gloria Steinem also exposed those men who had anything but what the bride may have expected. Some women don't mind living in the kitchen and enjoy being a mother of many children. That may or may not have been the life they willingly choose. Others never thought that was a requirement of love and marriage.

Steinem, a natural leader, used her wit to turn the tables on male domination. "A woman without a man is like a fish without a bicycle," she famously said. Her amusing quip was a play on a well-known song lyric: "A woman without a man is like a ship without a sail." Both quips may bring a smile, as the original demonstrates so clearly how past beliefs about women had men convinced they were, by nature, superior to women. How fulfilling for men to trust that females leaned on them for all of life's questions and answers. Or was it?

Steinem must have put aside her own reservations in order to initiate the excitement that eventually changed the lives of women. Gloria Steinem ended the mockery of thousands who saw the women's rights movement as something that would forever be a huge joke.

Although she could have easily taken care of her own destiny, Steinem was fighting for a larger cause, and she needed a lot of other females to fight the fight along with her. And they did!

Gloria was sharp, energetic, and goal-oriented. She entered Smith College as a young woman and both earned a Phi Beta Kappa key and graduated magna cum laude. Importantly too, she accepted a Chester Bowles Fellowship to India, where she was excited to study Mahatma Gandhi's way of developing a grass roots organization. Acting upon what she learned in India, she put her plans for Women's Liberation in motion.

Proliferation of her ideas accelerated, and enthusiasm for them grew rapidly. Her name and ideas took hold, and in 1995, Steinem won a Lifetime Achievement Award from *Parenting* magazine and was lauded by *Biography* magazine, which listed her as one of the most influential women in America. With this sudden energy surrounding Steinem, her list of awards grew longer and longer. Eventually,

President Barack Obama reached out to her, acknowledging her accomplishments by awarding her the Presidential Medal of Freedom, the highest civilian honor in the United States.

Excitingly, Gloria Steinem married for the first time when she was sixty-six years old. She wed sixty-one-year-old David Bale, a South African-born entrepreneur on September 3, 2000. Better known than him was his son, actor Christian Bale.

After years of being an uncompromising, independent woman, Steinem rounded out her life. Unfortunately, as life can do, David died from a brain lymphoma on January 3, 2004. Steinem stood by her husband while making sure he got the best of care at the Santa Monica Health Care Center until his life was over that November.

By nature, Steinem was forever strong. She went on to appear live in the CBS television show *The Good Wife*, where her character encouraged the lead character Alicia Florick to accept the opportunity to run for the Illinois State Attorney's office. Certainly that is what Gloria Steinem would have done in a real campaign. However, when Florick stepped out to accept the position offered to her, she quickly realized she had only been used. Although she believed the male political establishment was behind her, it was simply a front. What a way for the CBS / *The Good Wife's* writers to get Steinem's long, arduous fight to support females to historically go bad. Like so many other females in politics, the shows main character was quickly pushed aside. Chicago's male political establishment symbolically threw her to the ground and ended Alicia Florick's dream.

Yes. Gloria Steinem fought the fight against male domination on the job and in politics when lesser women would have quit championing competent females. Gloria never quit supporting her goals for women. She had the strength to stay the course and meet both those who were for her women's rights movement and those against it face-to-face! And seldom did those compelling females behind this revolutionary cause ever weaken beneath her encouragement. The fact remains that no one has done more for women than Gloria Steinem!

Gloria Steinem's analysis of the circumstances of females

informed her that it was an issue she could not overlook. She was smart, potently tough, and dedicated to her cause. She stepped out at the right time—and timing is everything. Over time, there had been other female leaders, but Steinem persisted and soldiered on.

There had been other suffragettes, but their plans were not timely. Steinem outlasted her naysayers and gifted those who believed she could change their lives. Certainly, Gloria Steinem has been unusual, in the sense that she bequeathed a gift to women with their now historically successful opportunities.

Without the ability to swallow insults privately and sometimes publicly, she would not have been this persuasive trailblazer she was. For tough women swallow hard and stand their ground valiantly in spite of personal insults.

Woman must never melt with tears or pitch their anger to its heights. Isn't that anger expected only from men?

Strength comes from deep within people's brains and hearts, whether they are soldiers at war or females at work, who stand their ground, often facing great personal risk. Gloria Steinem implemented change for American women because she thought it was urgently needed. Perhaps other parts of the world will soon recognize that women and men should enjoy equal rights.

23

Christine Lagarde Serves the World By Representing 189 Countries

In 2013, at fifty-seven years old, Christine Lagarde was elected to lead the International Monetary Fund from its home base in Washington, DC. Born in Paris, Christine grew to be nearly six feet tall and professionally never stopped gaining successes. She reached higher and higher in order to continue her faith in the countries she served. She seemed made for the demands she was to encounter and the challenges she was to respond to.

Lagarde's 2013 election to guide the International Monetary Fund was an amazing achievement. A well-known lawyer, Lagarde was truly knowledgeable of the financial world's behaviors. By 2016, Lagarde was a popular leader to the worldwide community, where she represented 189 member countries.

That position didn't just fall into her lap; it was the result of a long history of experience. Much of her competitiveness began when she was a child. In France, the young Lagarde was a Girl Guide, which is very much the same as being a Girl Scout in the United States. There, she learned to swim and even successfully compete as a swimmer. That early background alone portrays the spunk she had as a young girl. In fact, she was so successful she became a member of the French national synchronized swimming team!

While her father died when she was young, Lagarde leaned on her mother for inspiration for her developing plans. Deep thinking helped Christine be accepted to the Holton-Arms School, a preparatory school for girls in Bethesda, Maryland. Leaving Bethesda after that first year in the United States, Christine set out to travel the United States in order to ascertain more about America.

Her preparedness came not only from her mother but also from her grandmother. With her father gone by the time she turned sixteen, Christine watched her mother take care of the entire family. Perhaps while witnessing her mother do everything, she learned to carry on that same energy as she went forward. She actively works today to advise those in other countries how to move successfully forward with the help of the International Monetary Fund.

While working out of her home base in DC, she encourages the appropriate visitors to visit either one or both of the fund's two buildings. Visitors must have appropriate ID's to take a look around either Building 1 or Building 2.

Globally, Christine is, in some senses, the parent to the world, in the image of her own mother's loyalty to her family when Christine's father died. Simply said, she accepted her position as if she had been elected Mother Earth.

During her world travels, Lagarde "has urged monetary cooperation country by country as needed, discussed international trade, and taught each country how to raise its levels of employment." The fund's goal is to aid countries so that they may one day be capable of reducing poverty and bleakness.

With the creation of the IMF in 1945, a massive plan for the fund to become the world's banker went forward. Astoundingly, Lagarde was elected to replace the far from wise Dominique Strauss-Kahn, who resigned after assaulting a female hotel employee in New York. Then just as quickly, he was found to (allegedly at that time) have participated in a prostitution ring in France.

With a grand sense of humor, Christine Lagarde has smiled when suggesting that if Lehman Brothers (a US financial institution that failed) had been the Lehman Sisters, it might not have imploded.

Christine has been in banking and law for many years. Both she and Supreme Court Justice Sandra Day O'Connor could look back to a time when, as new lawyers, neither of them could be hired unless they agreed to accept work as assistants to lawyers.

Whether or not her most recent term in office continues, Lagarde has been seen as a superlative manager who has fulfilled many of the IMF's goals. There has been some criticism because Dominique Strauss-Kahn and Christine Lagarde are both French. But Lagarde would be difficult to replace by a frontrunner from any country. She knows how to behave and looks great carrying out the fund's needs. The short list says she is well spoken, knows how to dress without overdoing her good taste, and wears low-heeled shoes. When possible, Lagarde spends time at her home in Normandy, France, with her family.

Who would argue that Christine Lagarde has not successfully been a godmother to her family and to the world? Although Lagarde seems to handle the world without offending, she is an intensely resilient, tough, exacting woman. She travels far and wide without tiring of serving others, and according to her own remarks, she seems to have either inherited her mother's genetics or simply learned never to allow minor things to bother her.

Additionally, her stamina is legendary. And aging beautifully, her short, gray hair is striking; she can speak like a professional while looking stunning.

Importantly, Lagarde's access to influential leaders around the world has helped her. But more essential is her willingness to seek others' thoughts before making challenging decisions. After all, the best family upbringing or the highest intelligence scores never say it all.

Lagarde's sinewy nature suggests she should again lead the International Monetary Fund. It is clear to most that the world's developing countries could not be in better hands than those of

Christine Lagarde. How could anyone replace her savvy, intelligence, and stamina?

Lagarde's leadership makes clear the depth of her commitment. Her facial expressions display a confidence that telegraphs her power to lead. Is there really another woman (or man) who can live up to her global work for the International Monetary Fund?

24

$\mathcal{S}$allie Krawcheck, Once the Victim, Is Back Again

I f ever a well-known woman was suddenly fired following her huge successes at a handful of wealth management leadership positions on Wall Street, it was Sallie Krawcheck. Of course, it all precipitated on the back of the 2008 US financial debacle! No matter that her competency was well known and praise for her abounded, Krawcheck was ousted abruptly from the Bank of America / Merrill Lynch wealth management division, where she held the position of chief financial officer. Actually, it appears that she was the scapegoat for the Bank of America's Chairman of the Board Brian Moynihan. When United States' investments plunged to the bottom of financial charts nearly everywhere, Moynihan was apparently never touched himself. He kept his position at the bank.

Excitingly and bravely, after her forced exit from her Bank of America success, Sallie had the courage to brush herself off and start all over again. Certainly her conduct did not follow that of the men who stayed. For in fact, the top men at brokerage firms remained in deep financial trouble but, in most cases, were not fired between 2008 and 2010. Those people who believed in Sallie Krawcheck had known she was too strong to fail. After all, she had been a scapegoat for Bank of America's failure. Most saw her plight as that of a popular victim, while she was a decent, intelligent Wall Street success.

For outsiders and insiders alike, it took little thinking to believe that Krawcheck lost her job because she was a woman who could surpass and outclass most men! Women picked up on this unfairness quickly. Traditionally, the men in charge had the habit of blaming women for their own errors. A woman in a man's world often covered up or took the blame for their bosses' catastrophes.

Sallie Krawcheck was known by many in the business as the best wealth manager in the country. Implausibly, it was she who lost her job at Bank of America while numerous males stayed, still awarded large sums of money, and watched her "train wreck." The leadership simply called this restructuring. However, while Krawcheck's wealth management positions and superior investment reputation was erased, she says she earned "the dubious distinction of having worked for seven financial services CEOs."

Sallie's circumstances were embarrassing, as well as unfathomable. And during this period, she was labeled by others across the financial world as "the most honest broker on Wall Street." Yes! Krawcheck was a genuine person. And no doubt many other moneyed professionals might never have thought to choose honesty over dishonesty during these failing times. But with that committed praise, Krawcheck knew somehow she would find her way back to the top.

Krawcheck became truly vulnerable when she stuck her neck out during this recession to speak directly to Bank of America's board of directors. She explained that she believed it was the bank's moral responsibility to reimburse clients for flopped investments. Her comments opened her up to exacting criticism. In other words, the bank's leadership wanted no part of such honesty.

While Sallie believed these clients should be reimbursed for losses incurred as a result of poorly advised investments, she must have known that no good deed goes unpunished.

Unfortunately, this well-intentioned wealth management guru and properly reared Charleston, South Carolina, girl had faced her male colleagues erringly and ended up shooting herself right in the foot. If nothing else, her quick rejection must have awakened her to the underlying, unstated jealousy of those who led Bank of America to quickly bring her success to a close.

Today, many would say that Sallie, a beauty at that, was fired both because she was a woman and because she "erroneously" suggested a bit of financial mercy for those investors who had lost substantial parts of their retirement savings because of bad times. Deeper still, there remained the small investors who had been given bad investment advice by some of those Bank of America advisers.

But Krawcheck was known to be capable, and turned things around and gave herself a new start: Fairly quickly after being fired, she bought 85 Broads, a global organization that at the time had a membership of thirty thousand women. The name pointed to the organization's address—on New York's Broad Street—while also being heartwarming for Sallie. After all, she had grown up close to Broad Street in her hometown of Charleston, South Carolina.

There, history frames an intersection known as "The Four Corners of Law." That Broad Street intersection represents a history of stability, witnessed by edifices representing federal, state, city, and church. The corner's buildings include the courthouse (state law), City Hall (municipal law), the Federal Building with its post office (federal law), and Saint Michael's Episcopal Church (canon law). What better influence could the young Krawcheck have grown up with than the wealth of history in her hometown of Charleston, South Carolina?

Smart as always, Krawcheck went on to become the chair of Ellevate Network (formerly 85 Broads), a global network for professional women. Then she founded Ellevest, a digital investment platform for women, to support the growing interest of female investors. She is known for having a world of financial information.

Sallie's devotion to female investors has grown. As always, she remains a strong, forward-moving force for others.

Sallie is devoted to reaching more people. She, as always, believes in supporting others' successful investment potential. She knows that women are capable of success due to their ability to listen, learn, and work hard to determine their financial paths.

In 591 BC, Heraclitus remarked, "Everything flows, nothing stands still." Indeed, bright women and men know that nothing stands still. Krawcheck must have quickly shed a few tears before acknowledging this truth—circumstances are always changing. She didn't grind to a halt. She wiped away her tears and pressed forward to face the future. And there she became "successful Sallie," at the top of the business world again.

This lovely Charleston girl always had a lot of abilities. She was smart, funny, and born with the ability to be special.

She was a high school cheerleader as a girl; was an outstanding track star in South Carolina; and as a high school senior, was honored with a South Carolina Presidential Scholarship. She also received a Morehead Scholarship to attend the University of North Carolina, where she graduated from the school's journalism program. Going further, she obtained an MBA in 1992 from Columbia University, graduating Beta Gamma Sigma.

Her family includes her husband and their two children. Her husband is also a professional, and when the children were young, the pair decided to alternate days in order to make sure one of the parents were always with the children.

Obviously, Krawcheck's world moves fast. Yet she is always effective in the ever-changing times. As a couple, those times depend on both of them.

Who has most recently appeared on the horizon of the banking world but a young female who is similar to Krawcheck in that she has what it takes to succeed in our always complicated world?

Natalie Clark at fifteen years old was featured in the *Wall Street Journal* as a strong, thinking girl. At fifteen and the owner of five thousand shares of Bank of America stock given to her by her grandparents, brave Natalie stood up at a Bank of America shareholders meeting to question Chief Executive Brian Moynihan about the declining value of her five thousand shares.

Clark pointed out in front of hundreds of other investors that her grandparents had left her those shares so she could attend college.

Stop now! It's important to point out that Clark was addressing the very same Moynihan who fired Sallie Krawcheck and apparently stayed on in his position, even though his leadership has never successfully brought back much of its stocks value. Could this mean that the good ol' boy network is still in control?

As women learn younger and younger about financial markets, as well as taking charge of their lives rather than giving up and letting men do their thinking for them, both women and men should wind up happier. As women learn younger about investments and finances, there will be more Sallie Krawchecks and more women who will be saved by their own knowledge. And no one doubts that the young Natalie Clark will be one of them.

Whether it is Sallie or Natalie showing the way, the message is clear: one must be a fighter to stand up for what's right and speak out against what is wrong and to win.

Nothing ever stays the same. Krawcheck's family, intelligence, and education fortified her faith in staying the course when things went wrong. Those three things mean everything for women with goals. What strong people don't have goals and set their sights on achieving them? However, a woman's toughness is internal, seldom seen outwardly but always useful, if not lifesaving.

To be publically humiliated as Sallie Krawcheck was by Bank of America and, nevertheless, have the ability to recover quickly and go forward again, she must get an A+. After all that's happened, she is still Sally Krawcheck—lovely, kind, intelligent, admired, and now better and even more successful that ever.

Sources

1. Boudicca, queen of the Iceni people in Eastern England, died in AD 61. *Wikipedia, Wiki*; Queen Boudicca; *The History of Rome* (Charles Scribner's Sons, 1978), 284.
2. Elizabeth I lived from 1533 to 1603. *Wikipedia, Wiki*; Elizabeth I, *English Social History* (W. W. Norton and Co. Inc., 1987).
3. Israeli prime minister from 1969 to 1974, Golda Meir died at eighty years old in 1978 in Jerusalem, Israel. *Wikipedia, Wiki*. Golda Meir was Israel's PM who immigrated first to Milwaukee, Wisconsin, where she became an active Zionist. Biography.com.
4. Margaret Thatcher served three terms as England's prime minister. She died in 2013 at eighty-seven years old. Biography.com editors, "Margaret Thatcher Biography," A&E Television Networks, http://www.biography .com/people/margaret-thatcher-9504796; Margaret Thatcher, *The Path to Power* (1995).
5. Angela Merkel was born in 1954 and became the leader of the European Union through 2016. www.biography.com. She is the current leader of the Christian Democratic Union and chancellor of Germany.
6. Benazir Bhutto, the eleventh prime minister of Pakistan, was assassinated on December 27, 2007, at age fifty-four. *Wikipedia, Wiki*. Benazir Bhutto, Women's History, history.com.
7. Indira Gandhi was India's only female prime minister and the only child of Mahatma Gandhi. *Wikipedia, Wiki*. Indira Gandhi, Facts & Summary, history.com.
8. Malala Yousafzai, biographical, Nobelprize.org; Malala Yousafzai, *Wikipedia, Wiki*.
9. Anne Frank lived from June 12, 1929, to February or March 1945. *Wikipedia, Wiki*. The Diary of Anne Frank's Annex Diary Letters from June 14, 1942, to August 1, 1944.

10. Sybil Ludington (April 5, 1761, to February 26, 1839) went beyond the efforts of Paul Revere. *Wikipedia, Wiki.* Sybil Ludington, "The Making of a Revolutionary War Hero," *New England Quarterly* 88 (June 2015).

11. John Milton, *Paradise Lost* (Publishing Co.: New York, 1957), 73–515. Find also Milton's epic poem in blank verse on *Wikipedia, Wiki.*

12. Kate Chopin, *The Awakening* (1899); *Wikipedia, Wiki.* Kate Chopin was a woman with different lifestyles, who included Southern culture in her book and history. *Wikipedia, Wiki.*

13. Charlotte Perkins Gilman, "The Yellow Wallpaper" (1892). Gilman's famous work exposed the faults of the then popular "rest cure." *Wikipedia.org.* "The Yellow Wallpaper" is within the author's home library, and she has kept this playbook's script for acting in competitions in both 1957 and 1959 until present; also commercial artist and lecturer. *Wikipedia.org.*

14. Amelia Earhart was born on July 24, 1897, and disappeared on July 2, 1937. She was an aviation pioneer. *Wikipedia, Wiki. What Happened to Amelia Earhart?* History.com.

15. Danica Patrick, born March 25, 1982, is an American professional stock car driver. Fox Sports Channel. A keynote speaker often seen on television, Patrick often visits applauding girls on race days. Fox Sports Channel.

16. Shirley Chisholm, born November 1924, was, in 1968, the first African American woman elected to the United States Congress. *Wikipedia.org*; Shirley Chisholm, Facts & Summary, history.com.

17. Zora Neale Hurston, born in 1937, is best known to the world for *Their Eyes Were Watching God*, Britannica.com, and Zora Neale Hurston, folklorist, American Author, Britannica.com.

18. Oprah Winfrey, born in 1954, was molested in childhood but saved by her father. *Wikipedia, Wiki.* She is a well-known author and talk show host, *Wikipedia, Wiki.*

19. Ayaan Hirsi Ali, born in 1969, is a writer and former Dutch politician. *Wikipedia, Wiki.* Ayann Hirsi Ali, *Heretic: Why Islam Needs a Reformation Now* (2015).

20. Azar Nafisi, born in 1955, is a writer and professor who changed her citizenship from Iranian to American in 2008. *Wikipedia, Wiki.* Azar Nafisi, *Reading Lolita in Iran.*

21. Sandra Day O'Connor served as associate justice of the US Supreme Court from 1981 until her retirement in 2006. *Wikipedia, Wiki.* O'Connor grew up working on her family ranch. *Wikipedia, Wiki.*

22. Gloria Steinem, born in 1934, was an American feminist, journalist, and social and political activist. She still works for women, as seen in her cameo on 2016's CBS television series *The Good Wife.*

23. Christine Lagarde, born in 1956, is the managing director of the International Monetary Fund. In the French government, she was minister of Economic Affairs, Finance, and Employment.

24. Sallie Krawcheck, born in 1964, is the chair of Ellevest and the owner of Ellevate Network. She was once the president of the global wealth and investment management division of Bank of America. *wikipedia.org.*

Printed in the United States
By Bookmasters